OUTREACH:

God's Miracle Business

OUTREACH:
God's
Miracle
Business

Elvis Marcum

BROADMAN PRESS • NASHVILLE, TENNESSEE

To
the membership of Graceland Baptist Church
who has dared to dream
with their pastor . . .
and has seen those dreams
become realities

Library of Congress Catalog Card Number: 75-10507
Dewey Decimal Classification: 254
Printed in the United States of America

FOREWORD

I first met Elvis Marcum in the fall of 1966. I had assumed my responsibilities as the first Billy Graham Professor of Evangelism at Southern Baptist Theological Seminary in Louisville, Kentucky.

Having just spent a year in New York City studying the church in urban America, I was much more aware of the basic questions being asked than I was of the answers. Consequently, my first class on "Evangelism in the City" had a thick bibliography, lots of reading assignments, an enormous term project, and a great deal of rabbit-chasing type of discussion. The one thing that I was absolutely sure of was that the church through the gospel that it shares, the fellowship that it experiences, and the ministry it is capable of performing has to play a more important role in the days ahead. I was also convinced that "business as usual" was impossible for the future.

Elvis Marcum, the author of this book, was in that first class. About a month into the class he made an appointment and came to see me in my office. I honestly think he came to drop the course and for good reasons. He said: "Dr. Chafin, I need this course more than anyone there, but I am afraid I won't be able to keep up with the reading assignments and projects because of the responsibilities of my church in southern Indiana."

I ascertained from talking with him a deep commitment and profound seriousness about the church in the city. I am not sure what Dean St. Amant would have thought, but I made Elvis an offer he was unable to turn down. I assured him that if he attended the class, read the assignments, and took the tests that I would see that he had a passing grade. He stayed in the class, relaxed a bit, and made a solid student. As it turned out, the one student who considered dropping the class has done more with the church in the city than any other student in the class.

About four months after completing this class, Elvis Marcum showed up in my office with an area missionary from southern Indiana and a "dream" for using two or three Southern Seminary students in some "house-church" type ministry in the inner city of New Albany. I worked with him and the missionary in initiating this program and enlisted and helped supervise the first couples. This was the beginning of a whole new day at Graceland Baptist Church.

To some degree New Albany is a unique community and Graceland Baptist Church is a unique church. A superficial copying of programs or styles of leadership would be very unwise, but there is a degree to which Graceland is not unique at all. It is an example of what a pastor and people can do if they are willing to decide honestly that they will become "all things to all men if by any means they may save some."

I commend this pastor, this people, and this book to you.

KENNETH L. CHAFIN
South Main Baptist Church
Houston, Texas

Introduction

From the time Graceland began to unfold as a miracle of God's outreach, I stood amazed that I could have a part. Soon after I realized what God was doing, I wanted to share it with others—not in order to boast, but to magnify Christ and to motivate other churches.

I believed then, as I do now, that what God has done in our church, he wants to do in hundreds of churches—thousands of churches. The desire to relate this story is for the glory of God, who indeed is in the *miracle business.*

Around two years ago the church asked me to write the story and gave me time aside for the purpose. My wife and I spent a month in Florida by the oceanside. During a part of each day we relaxed and rested. The remainder of the day I tried to put the story on paper. Out of that month, this book was conceived.

Since the story is in reality the story of those who make up the church—men, women, youth—I have asked them to help me with the account. This explains the unusual format of the book: personal accounts of the growth and development of our multiple ministries. The ministries are designed to reach people for Christ, but they are best shared by those who themselves were involved in their creation. And continue to be involved.

The book not only relates a story, but it answers how and why. Our humble prayer is that this book will give you ideas about church growth and outreach. It is not enough for us to share blessings with you, unless we want you to experience those same blessings for you and your church. Throughout the book

I have included many names of those who have participated in God's miracle business. This is to keep a strong personal flavor.

Imagine yourself sitting in the middle of a sharing group, as we discuss what God has done for us, and what he can do for you. No church, including Graceland, has a corner on God's power. All that God requests is that we make ourselves available to him. And dream of miracles. And believe that God will perform them.

I want to thank all of those who have had a part in putting this book together. Dr. Kenneth L. Chafin helped us institute many of our innovative ministries at Graceland. Thanks to him for his lasting influence in my life and the life of our church. We appreciate his writing the *Foreword* to the book.

Special thanks are due to Dr. Eugene Skelton of the Baptist Sunday School Board. He has given me consultation and valuable suggestions. The entire book, of course, expresses thanks to God and to the members of Graceland Baptist Church.

Elvis Marcum
New Albany, Indiana

CONTENTS

1
What Happens at Graceland?

In May, 1974, the Sunday School Department of the Convention of Baptists in Indiana and the Sunday School Department of the Baptist Sunday School Board conducted a bus clinic at Graceland Baptist Church. Those attending not only participated in conferences through the week, but accompanied the Graceland bus workers on their Saturday visits and participated in the worship services on Sunday. One of those attending later described his impressions of Graceland.

Eugene Skelton: "To visit the Graceland Baptist Church of New Albany, Indiana, is an experience to be remembered. To be talked about later. And to be repeated. But most of all, it is an experience to be enjoyed. For joy is one of the real words, if not the very best word, to describe this vibrantly alive church.

"You know about the church, maybe a great deal about it, before you visit. You've read about it in one of the leadership magazines, or *Outreach*, or *Home Missions* magazine, or the *Brotherhood Builder.*

"If you're not a Southern Baptist, you may have read about it in your own denomination's publication, such as *The General Baptist Messenger.* Whether a Baptist or not, you will probably know about the church; you've read stories of its work in such daily metropolitan newspapers as *The Louisville Times* and the *Louisville Courier-Journal* or in *The Evansville Press* or *The New Albany Tribune.* If you've been in New Albany as long as a day someone's told you about the church and you've seen its buses. How could you miss them? They go places every day helping people do things they could not do otherwise.

"Yet, even if someone has told you what to expect, you are not prepared for the experience of visiting at Graceland. To properly begin a Sunday at the church, you must go early. Seven o'clock in the morning. That's when the church staff gathers to pray. Join them; you'll be welcomed. Sure, it's early; most people are just stirring and turning over for a few minutes more sleep, or maybe for another hour or so. Even most of those who will have a full day's activity in their churches usually have not begun to move about yet. But it's a good time to pray. To thank God for the day—whether it's a day of sunshine, or already has begun with rain or sleet or snow—and to praise God for the miracles he will bring to pass in the church that day.

"As for that, the pastor and his wife already have spent an earlier hour—beginning at six o'clock in the morning—in the church prayer bus. Others have slipped in and out of the bus all through the night.

"So at seven o'clock your day at Graceland has begun. It will be a busy day. A victorious day. And remember? A day of joy. Between the prayer time and the first worship service, grab a cup of coffee. Maybe a doughnut. You'll find them in the kitchen, prepared for bus workers and others. But hurry; the first worship service is at 8:30; less than an hour away.

"An expectant group gathers in the auditorium for this service. Although the auditorium may not be filled, the spirit of worship will be present. The choir is robed and half-fills the choir space. The music is happy and enthusiastic. The pastor's message is warm and appealing. At the conclusion of the message an invitation is extended and several people respond. Most likely, these are persons who through the previous week—or weeks—have been touched by one or more of the many ministries of the church. Each time the church touches the life of a person, it turns him toward Bible study and to Christ as Savior and Lord.

"The spirit of happiness is evident, and it carries through from the first worship to the hour that follows, the hour of Bible study. By the time you leave the auditorium and arrive at the parking areas surrounding the church building, the buses have begun to swing into the church yard from the bus barn several miles away. The barn is on the site of the new 'Abundant Life Community.'

"More about that later. Workers have begun to find their places on the buses which will be theirs to use for the morning. For the next half-hour to forty-five minutes the happiness you felt in the worship service is mixed with excitement as one after another of the buses leave, carrying many people many places on differing missions, all connected with Bible study. Did you notice that everyone seems to smile? Everyone does. It is evidence of the happy anticipation they feel as they go to minister to people throughout the church area.

"Ride one of the buses. Any one. Climb aboard and take a seat near the front. The bus captain may explain his mission for the day as you swing down out of the church yard and into the main street. He may go from house to house, street by street, gathering riders. Are you seeing that he never waits for any rider just to come to the bus; he steps off and greets each by name, given name. Almost from the time the first riders board the bus, there is singing; the bus captain believes the time spent in riding can be joy-filled and useful in witnessing. If his bus fills largely with junior-high-age youth, he will swing by the church to discharge his younger and older riders and then head to the nearby junior high school where his remaining riders will experience Bible study and youth worship this morning. Don't leave; stay with them. You'll be glad you did.

"But your bus may have gone an entirely different route. It may have gone to a nursing home and gathered a group in wheel chairs, then transporting them to the church for Bible study and worship. They'll sit together on the right side of the church at the later worship. Or your bus may travel to a large housing development. If it does, be prepared for what will take place. The bus stops and the workers go into the recreation room. Soon a group gathers for Bible study, for Sunday School.

This Sunday School group will conclude in time for the workers and others to board the waiting bus and arrive at the church in time for the late worship.

"If you let these go by, you may board a bus that just stops at a street corner far away from the church. Immediately, several teen-agers leave the bus and begin going from house to house. What are they doing? Wait. You'll understand. And you do—when you see people begin to come from the houses and move toward the bus. Look. The bus captain is preparing to set up a Bible class on the bus. This bus, too, will leave its street-corner location and take the workers, and any others who desire, to the church for the worship service at eleven o'clock.

"Did you decide just to watch the buses leave, while you remained at the church? If so, when the last bus is gone, find a Sunday School class. A class for your age group. Since the Sunday School is fully graded and organized with Preschool, Children's, and Adult departments meeting at the church, this will be easy. There is an auditorium class for those who have not yet found a place in one of the traditionally-organized departments and classes. There is also an in-progress department—or class, if you please—for potential Sunday School workers.

"Before you settle into a class, look around. Every classroom seems to be filled; many are overflowing. You know already that a giant Sunday School enlargement effort is projected for several months in the future. Where, you wonder, will all the new classes and departments find places to meet? Ask someone. He'll tell you: God will provide another miracle to care for the people.

"Don't leave now; stay for the worship service following the Bible study hour. And don't delay about getting into the auditorium. Every seat will be taken.

"You watch the people crowd in. The auditorium is filled. From wall to wall and all the way to the back. The balcony also is full, from the railing in front to the wall at the back. Strange—since another worship service for youth is in progress just a few blocks away.

"Find a seat. You might feel wedged in when the pew fills up, but don't be concerned about that. It's part of the joy of being in Graceland for the day.

"The choir enters and fills the loft. Not a space is available for another singer. The theme of the music is the joy and vibrancy of serving Christ. Prayers are offered and the choir responds. The theme of the response is expectation that miracles will follow as answers to offered petitions. The pastor comes to speak.

"His preaching is not loud and his sermon is not sophisticated; he comes as person-to-person and his message is as heart-to-heart. He speaks of Christ, presenting the simple gospel in a way that all may understand. People respond.

"Their response is seen in the eager attention they give, heard in the murmured "Amens" from time to time from all parts of the congregation, and felt as several make their way to the front with the singing of the invitation. Those who are received into the church fellowship, as was true at the earlier service, in the main have already been touched by one or more of the church's ministries.

"When the service ends, don't hurry away. Not that you could, even if you wanted to do so. The people will hold you long enough to learn who you are and to welcome you to their church. If you stand and listen, they'll tell you something of the church, what it is today, what it has been, but most of all what they hope it becomes."

A New Testament church is made up of God's people joined in a mission to the world. Graceland, like many churches, has been blessed with some of God's choice people. In the earlier days the then tiny church prayed that God would send some of these not only "into Macedonia," but "into New Albany to help us." With the coming of Bob and Helen Burton that prayer was answered in a marvellous manner. Let them share the story of their experience at Graceland, telling what the church has meant to them.

Mrs. Helen Burton:

"My husband and I started coming to Graceland in August, 1954. We had moved to New Albany two years earlier and had visited another church. But we were not happy with that church and didn't go for two years. A couple of men from Graceland came to visit us; we visited the church. We continued to attend for three or four months. We made up our minds we wanted to serve the Lord here and joined. We came into the church.

"In about six weeks the pastor called and asked me to teach a Sunday School class. I had never done this—in fact the church we came from would not permit a woman to teach a class. I had never had a woman Sunday School teacher. The pastor came to see me two or three times and I prayed about the challenge. I decided I would do my best if the Lord would help me. I consented to teach.

"I enjoy teaching. I started with Preschoolers; then after two or three years I moved up to the younger Children; then I went to the older Children. I taught Children for eight or ten years and then decided I needed to be taught for a while. I went into Mrs. Marcum's class and was there for about three years. Got too old and had to go out, so I started teaching again.

"Now I teach fourth grade girls. We go down to Hazelwood school. We don't have enough room here so we go there on buses and we go down there and teach. I have also been in the church choir for twelve years.

"The church has been such a blessing to our lives, my husband and myself. At first we had a pretty rough time. I know many times when I was serving as janitor I've hung out these windows trying to clean them. We even had to pay for our own literature that we used in our Sunday School classes. But in the past twelve years everything has grown so fast; it has just been a miracle."

Bob Burton also speaks of what happens at Graceland and of the profound effect the church has had on his life.

* * *

Now I'll pick up the narrative.—E.M.

In the Spring of 1963 I became involved in the life of the Graceland Mission. One afternoon just before college graduation I arrived home to meet my wife with a letter in her hand. The letter asked if I wanted to move to New Albany. Our first reaction was of little interest to the situation. We were happy in the church we were serving and did not think of leaving at that time. We prayed about the situation and left it in the hands of God. All the while we had nagging thoughts, "Maybe we should go see, it won't hurt to go visit, maybe we should go, maybe this is God opening a door of service to us." A few days later we found ourselves on a visit to New Albany. It was an exciting visit, as we drove through the city and saw the tremendous opportunity that was here. What a challenge! What a need! Immediately our hearts were open to God's leadership in coming to New Albany.

All the way home we talked about the matter and the things that could be done. We were excited about the place, but we did not know for sure it was God's will for us to leave the church we were serving. We decided to pray that if it were God's will for us to move to New Albany that he would open the door. And this is what he did. A few days went by. Then a call came for us to meet with the pastor of the Beechmont Baptist Church for an interview.

A few months later we were loading our furniture on a "U-Haul-It" truck and heading north. We arrived in New Albany with a sense of excitement concerning the new field.

The excitement of the moment was soon to be overshadowed by the sadness of the situation. The parsonage spoke concerning the need of the Mission. The doors were in need of repair, the roof leaked, and the wall of one room moved in sympathy with the opening and closing of the door. The building showed the defeat of the small, struggling congregation.

Not only did the buildings speak of the spirit of defeat, but the records spoke loud and clear. The financial condition was deplorable. Payments on the buildings were equal to the total offering of the Mission. There were no gifts given to the mission causes through the Cooperative Program. The treasurer was under constant pressure because of the inadequate funds. Poor credit had caused a problem with the community. The Mission was heavily in debt and almost on the brink of despair. The Sunday School Board in Nashville had stopped sending any more literature, because we were behind in payments. Dr. L. C. Ray, a retired minister, wrote the Board and was able to get help for the literature.

The spiritual condition of the Mission was at low tide. There had not been a baptism for sixteen months. The Mission fellowship was not only "split"—it was "splintered." There were few capable leaders in the congregation. The few leaders that were present were more than willing to sacrifice time, talent, and money.

One of the Young People's leaders, a Seminary Student and now a foreign missionary, would gather his soft drink bottles along with a little change and get drinks for the young people's social.

The Mission was using all of its strength to survive. It was not attempting to reach out in the community. This was further evidenced by the spiritual apathy in the Sunday School. My first Sunday at Graceland found eighty-four (84) people in Sunday School, and less in the worship service. Of this number sixty percent were not affiliated with the Church.

There was little concept of a ministering body of Christ. Therefore, the community looked at Southern Baptists as a "sect" to be ignored or feared rather than to be respected and joined. A survey of several hundred houses showed a high percentage of the church community was affiliated with other denominations. Few were Baptist or had any desire to identify with Baptists.

The ministers in the community had already decided that it was impossible for the church to survive. There were too many churches in the community that were larger. Graceland did not have a chance of reaching the community (so they thought).

"One of the bright spots in the bleak situation was the discovery that half of the city was not affiliated with any church. The churches in the city were not reaching out to this segment of the community.

Nineteen-sixty-four, a year of doubt and decision. The first part of the year was lived under the shadow of defeat. Offerings were a little over $150 a week. No one to help with the music program, no money to provide help.

A meeting was called in March, 1964, to discuss the situation. Dr. Arthur Rutledge, presently Executive Secretary of the Home Mission Board, Beechmont Baptist Church's Mission Committee and Graceland's Mission Committee were present for the meeting. "What shall we do?" was in the minds of all present. One question was should we sell the building and move to another location? The reason was the inability to reach people from the community. Another idea was to refinance and give the Mission more money with which to operate the program. Another idea was to let the Mission become a church and accept more responsibility.

Out of that historic meeting came a ray of hope—a decision to refinance the building, and work toward the Mission becoming a church. Dr. Rutledge said he believed Graceland could become a self-supporting church of 250-300 in Sunday School and 500-600 members in the years to come. But it would be years before this could happen.

The March meeting to refinance and move toward establishing a church gave some inspiration to move forward. The Mission had begun to grow some numerically and financially. However, much was to be desired in program and building. Oftentimes we would be disappointed when a Southern Baptist would move into the city from a thriving church in the South, only to visit one or two times and then choose another church of a different denomination. The reason given was inadequate music, nursery, etc.

A little humor was often added to the services, not by intention but by accident. One morning as the invitation was being given, one of our deacons, who was sitting on a small pew in the back of the church, moved a little and to his dismay the pew collapsed; and he found himself sitting on the floor during the invitation.

August of 1964 was the beginning of a "New Day." The Mission was constituted into a church. Things were on the move and God provided a man to come and lead our music program. Bill Barnes and his wife Margie were called to head our music program. They lived several miles from the church and Sunday and Wednesday would drive 50 miles to the church. Bill had been a friend of mine in college. He was a music teacher in a high school. The church paid him a small salary for his services, but his tithe was quite a bit more than his salary. This shows how God works. He not only provided a man for the job—he also provided the resources. Bill and Margie loved the Lord and put many hours into the work of developing a choir.

Finally, one of our members decided we needed an organ. But there were no funds available to purchase one. So a plan was devised whereby we would use small wooden banks that looked like churches and give them to the members to save pennies for an organ payment. This we did. We purchased an organ and used the pennies to make the payments. One Sunday a month was set aside for the people to bring the banks to the church with their offerings. Needless to note, many people would forget to bring the banks and it became Bill's job to go and collect the money. Many people contributed more than the pennies and the organ was soon paid for. The organ was a splendid blessing to the spirit of the worship services.

But with every advancement there seemed to be a difficulty. Such as when our chairman of deacons and his family—all tithers, president of the WMU, Sunday School teachers and serving in many other positions—were transferred to Pennsylvania. When we heard this it seemed as if everything had dropped out from under us. And you can imagine our dismay when, on the Saturday night before the first Sunday in the new church year, the newly-elected Sunday School superintendent called and said he would not be back any more. He was a tither, youth worker, you name it. But God never leaves us in the middle of any difficulties without providing his promised help. Within a few days, one man in the church started giving more money than both of the men that left were giving, without knowing anything about the need their leaving had caused.

The year 1965 saw the beginning of a spiritual awakening. On the Fourth of July we began a revival which brought a number of new families into the church and a new sense of expectancy to those already there. God had begun a movement that was destined to reach the lives of hundreds of people and eventually change the church into one which believed that nothing was impossible to the believer.

The question, "Can anything good come out of Graceland?" changed to the question, "What does God intend for this church?" This was the difference God had wrought in the hearts and lives of the people.

Fred Bales of *The Louisville* (Kentucky) *Courier-Journal* and *Times* described the church as more than just a building. He took more than half a page in a Sunday edition of the paper to depict what he saw happening at Graceland.

Fred Bales:

"To find the Graceland Southern Baptist Church takes a lot more than going to the white-steepled brick building on Charleston Avenue in New Albany. The church is all over town. At Bono housing project, at a nearby high-rise housing facility over in the middle-class subdivision of Parkwood, in the Beechwood housing project. Yes, and back in the home church, where the auditorium fills twice for worship and also houses a Bible study class, while downstairs more than 150 youngsters sit in a worship service designed just for themselves. Not to mention worship in a nearby junior high school. Buses with a 'Follow Me to Church' sign painted on the back roll up to the doors to let off children and adults for these many activities of Bible study and worship."

What really happens at Graceland? What caused these things to happen? Can they happen at other churches, also? How can they happen there? These are the questions the remaining chapters of this book will answer.

2
People Are Prepared by God

What happens at Graceland? Perhaps the briefest and best way to answer this question is simply, "Lives are changed through the amazing grace of God." The multiple ministries of the church are the means through which God reaches out, first to touch a person's life through the care and concern of his people, and then to make that life over through the touch of his Holy Spirit.

Mrs. Bernice Young, a member of Graceland from its beginning, describes the life of the church as one miracle after another, but believes the greatest miracle of all is the one she and others have seen so many times—the miracle of the transformed life.

Bernice Young:

"Looking back to January, 1952, I think of the one-room building with a warm stove for heat and an old icebox with a cloth over it for a pulpit. I also think of the many miracles God has done for Graceland Southern Baptist Church.

"It took a miracle that first year to get our Vacation Bible School going. We had plenty of children, but few workers. Things seemed so difficult as to be impossible, but we left it to the Lord and moved ahead. He provided and we had a fine school. Another time we had so little money we couldn't pay our pastor. One of our members gave the money needed. Another miracle? Yes. God touched one of his children to do the impossible.

"I could name many other miracles—including God's sending our pastor to us. But the greatest of all miracles, and one I've seen happen many times, is seeing men and women, boys and girls saved. Lives really are changed at Graceland. The grace of the life-changing miracle work of God is seen here over and over again."

God Prepares the People

What makes the fellowship of Graceland unique and different from other places where I have served and ministered?

First of all, our people have dared to stand on the frontier of faith, they have discovered the wonder of God's provisions, they have been overwhelmed by the glory of the impossible, and they live with a sense of delight in the unusual.

Because of this fellowship and because they believe in this sort of ministry, they are not afraid to attempt things that many others would not attempt. They do not look at failure as falling down; they look at failure as *staying* down. They are not afraid to begin a new ministry, and if the ministry does not meet the needs of the community, then they simply change to another ministry.

We have taught our people to look for needs; wherever there is a need, God has a resource to meet that need. And when people are on the lookout for needs, needs are always showing up.

It is not unusual for a teacher in the high school to lead a young person to Christ. Only recently one of our teachers in the Jeffersonville, Indiana, High School led two of his students to the Lord. As I was working on this book, one of our teachers from Prosser Vocational High School walked into my office and talked about encouraging his students to sign up people for "Miracle Week," a special campaign in our church. And this same man leads his students to know the Lord Jesus Christ.

As we analyze what happens in a normal day in the lives of our congregation, we have to remark that "the church is everywhere." A reporter from *The Metropolitan News* observed, "It's the church all over town."

It intrigued me to hear what happened at a hamburger place in New Albany. One of the young men there talked with another who knew a couple of our ministers to young people. The young man asked, "What are they doing?" He had seen our young people come into the hamburger stand and pass out cards. Finally, the other fellow answered, "Why, they are ministers from Graceland, and they are just making a check with the young people." Really, I believe the guy with the questions thought that something illegal was going on—that our ministers were in the drug culture.

So, wherever you go, you see our people witnessing. Maybe this sharing consists of going out on Sunday morning, knocking on a door, and having a one-minute prayer meeting. On one occasion one of our men had knocked on a door just to speak to a person, have a short prayer, and let them know we were available. The lady said, "Well, I do need a loaf of bread. There hasn't been anyone visiting me for five years, and this morning I need a loaf of bread." This layman stopped his praying, met a need, came back with the bread, and then went on his way.

Some of our men move out into the community and have what we call "Mini Sunday School" classes. They conduct a short Sunday School class in which they teach the Bible on Sunday mornings to one or two people in a home.

One of our men was going about his bus schedule and he came across a little boy who was carrying a heavy sack of papers. The boy said, "This is just too heavy for me to carry—I'm in real need." So, the layman took time to carry the papers for the boy. Then, they went together to gather up other boys and girls for Sunday School. We see our people stirring on Sunday morning all across the city, whether it be a park, a recreational building, or sometimes a *rock* that is not occupied, and starting a class there.

So, we have taught our people that the church is everywhere. And Jesus Christ wants to meet human needs. But there is more than this—I feel that in the hearts of our people there is a dream so big that it takes the supernatural power of God to make that dream possible. If we have our usual negative attitudes, it's difficult for us to see the bigness of God. If we major on negatives, we are always looking at the things that cannot happen, rather than those that can happen.

When Jesus taught, "Nothing shall be impossible to you," he meant that we can have unlimited opportunities and unlimited faith. But people are at times overwhelmed by the bigness of the task. Yet, they must always be aware that God is bigger than any task.

When your purpose is bigger than your problems, you can have a sense of excitement. Most of the time, though, we tend to let our problems overshadow our purpose.

To forge ahead for Christ, believers cannot shy away from the difficult. God has helped our people to meet the difficult, the seemingly impossible situations, head-on. In our churches we often dream and have ideas—but then we seem afraid to venture on faith and attempt to reach the impossible. We are not like Joshua and Caleb who believed the children of Israel could walk in and conquer the land of Canaan. They challenged, "Let's take the land." We are more like the ten spies who protested, "There are giants in the land. We can't take the land."

Challenge the people. Challenge them to give their best. Motivate them to believe that God is "a God of might and miracles."

Do not be afraid to ask lay people to give. Out of giving they grew. And the more they give, the more they grow. As they give with gratitude, God blesses with his abundant grace and goodness. At Graceland our approach is simple—we encourage our people to use the abilities and talents that they have available.

We sum up each person's situation. What secular vocation does that person have? What training do they have in the workaday world? We capitalize on those abilities. We encourage them to use their training to communicate the gospel.

Mechanics work on the buses. Photographers communicate through pictures for the church, or work as roving photographers. If we have a publicity person in the church, we naturally use him in the publicity work of the church.

Nurses have a special touch for ministering in the name of

Christ. Businessmen have skills that keep our business affairs at the church running smoothly. We concentrate on finding out the skills of every person in the church, and we enlist those persons, with their talents, to minister for the church. That's not a complicated plan, is it? But it works to the glory of God. It proclaims the gospel through every possible means.

A man who teaches drama will soon be heading up a drama program for Graceland. He will also be in charge of lighting effects for our church auditorium. We have a man who works at the University of Louisville in video. What do you think he'll do here? All of our video work. He'll be working in the areas where he is trained.

What a tremendous impact this uncomplicated approach could have on countless churches. God gives talents to people. Why put a person in a work for which he has neither inclination nor skill? Suit the person, with his God-given gifts, to the task.

The challenge, of course, is always bigger than the man. We laughingly remark that at Graceland we try to challenge people as much as we can—and then add 10 percent! We believe that a Christian ought to stretch his horizons and faith. He has never quite arrived, and should never feel that he has. He should desire to become more like his Master—and that's a challenge, an exhilarating challenge!

Our lay people conduct a daily crusade against the ordinary. The church ought to be the most attractive place in the world. That is, it ought to be appealing to the Christian. We have fun, we laugh, we enjoy the fellowship. We call our church—for lack of a better expression—"one big, happy family."

I have often commented that even a flea has the intelligence to get off of a dead dog! And I am made to believe that a person should not be "punished" when he goes to church. And there are places where people are punished in the experience of going to church. That's unfortunate, because people attend church, hopefully, to gain strength for living, warm fellowship, and a worshipful experience.

Sometimes we in the churches almost defeat ourselves. It seems we're not really trying to serve the Lord. It's like the little boy who was standing by the fruit stand. A policeman asked him, "Are you trying to steal fruit?" The boy replied, "No sir, I'm trying not to!" And it seems that often we are struggling awfully hard not to serve the Lord. Beware of falling into the ruts. The status quo. The "same old thing."

Our people have tried to follow the spirit of the early Christians. Our people delight in doing the unusual—not doing it, though, for the sake of just doing the unusual. What we do is for that overriding purpose—reaching people for Christ.

We fully recognize that Jesus was not "a regular fellow." He was strikingly different. So, we as followers of Jesus must not beat the "beaten path" to death. We ask our people to strive to be creative. We believe that creativity is the mind of Christ in you, doing good. The work of Christ through you. We are to communicate the gospel in a creative way. We believe that the gospel never changes. Methods are always changing. Many of our laymen are constantly coming forth with new ideas, starting new ministries, moving away from the "ho hum" and the "hum drum."

There is an ever-present challenge before our people. Find new ways, better ways to minister. Our philosophy is: "The best way to do a thing hasn't been found, but we are seeking."

To move out for Christ, every church must have enthusiasm. We have an enthusiastic spirit at Graceland. We don't have a corner on enthusiasm. It is available to every believer and to every church. There is an excitement in our church. Enthusiasm comes from two Greek words, "en" and "theos"—meaning "in God." When we are in God, we ought to be enthusiastic. What a picture of God being in us through his Holy Spirit!

You will discover that there is a sense of expectancy, a creative approach to ministry, a spirit of enthusiasm. Our people are not afraid to fail, because in trying we may not always succeed. But even what we sometimes call *failure* can become a stepping stone to growth in Christ.

Another characteristic I have noticed about our people is their willingness, the commitment to give their best. Although I know there is no sacrifice we can give in the light of Jesus' sacrifice, we do ask our people to have a sacrificial spirit . . . to give something that costs something. I have observed hundreds of lay people being asked to give and give and give become the happiest people in the world.

It's out of giving the best that we have that God pours out the best that he has. Our sharing has enabled us to bless others, and in turn those blessings come back to us.

To summarize the spirit of our church—the people have a dream that is so big that the supernatural power of God is essential for the accomplishment. Our people are not afraid of the difficult, they stand on the frontier of faith. They have discovered the wonder of the impossible. They know that Jesus Christ can do anything; when they surrender their lives, they can stand in awe as God's marvelous purposes are worked out.

Yes, Graceland is a strange place. We stand in the land of miracles, and we expect miracles. We believe that the Word of God teaches us that the miraculous is God's way of showing the world that the supernatural is above the natural and that God is still on his throne.

God Prepares the Pastor

It was several years ago that the work of God was growing, but the *worker* was having difficulty. Although I knew what God had called me for, I did not have the joy of living I knew the Bible said a Christian should have. There was something lacking in my life. The vision was clear concerning the call of God, the people were coming in answer to prayer, but there was still this lack in my life. I was not quite ready for the responsibility of leading a church to achieve what God wanted for it.

In an unusual way God dealt with me. I was sitting in the office of Dr. Clyde T. Francisco, one of my professors at Southern Seminary in Louisville. Dr. Francisco had asked selected persons from congregations pastored by his students to evaluate their pastors. Dr. Francisco talked with me about the reports from several of my people. The reports were kind concerning my preaching and work, but this stood out. The people sensed my discouragement.

Dr. Francisco said, "When you go into the pulpit do not share your frustrations, fears, discouragements, and defeats. The people have all of these. Share the victorious way of the Lord Jesus Christ." This was great advice to me, advice well-received and practiced from that day forth.

Nevertheless, my inner life was not what I believed a minister should experience. I believed that the Bible taught abundant living. To be a Christian was challenging, but also an exciting, joyous journey of faith. Furthermore, I knew that showing was better than telling. My inner life was not measuring up to my basic convictions about the Christian experience.

I constantly lived in a struggle between what I read in God's Word and what I really experienced in living. Oftentimes my preaching was a duty, rather than a desire to proclaim God's Word. It seemed that no sooner had I finished one sermon that another one was due. I was always battling with time and groping for ideas. Sure, I studied hard, read widely, but I lacked warmth and readiness to preach with joy and expectancy.

The fall of 1966 found me still in the midst of the struggle for meaning. The last year of seminary did little to help this perplexed situation. I had a heavy load of required subjects. The church had grown to the extent that much was required in ministry. Questions were lingering in my mind—Is it worth the struggle? Does God intend for my ministry to be like this? What is the problem with me?

Midway of the semester I became ill and was taken to the hospital. For several days I lay in that hospital bed. I evaluated my work, my call to follow Jesus, my lack of power and purpose for living.

I remembered hearing Howard Butt, a wealthy layman, share in Seminary Chapel how his life had been changed. He talked about how he found the secret of trusting God without reservation. "I quit *trying* to be a Christian and started trusting Christ to do that for me, and my whole life changed." That's basically what he said.

This is exactly what I wanted to be able to do. Along with this layman's injunction to trust God, another influence began to take hold of my mind and heart. I had done a research paper on the work of the Holy Spirit. The truth I discovered in this time of study had been in my mind and was coming to fruition. The study revealed:

1. That God commanded all of his followers to be filled with the Holy Spirit (Eph. 5:22)
2. That the victorious life depended on the filling of the Holy Spirit (John 7:35)
3. That the work of Christ demanded that one be empowered with the Holy Spirit (Acts 1:8)

This is what I needed and desired for my life and work.

A few days after my soul-searching stay in the hospital, my wife and I found our way to the altar of the church one evening. I had spent many hours of self-examination in recent weeks and had found that my ministry had been carried on, to a great degree, in my own strength.

There at the altar together, my wife and I experienced an unusual closeness with God. I experienced a full surrender of my life to Jesus Christ. There was then a change in my attitude. A new power permeated my mind and heart. My faith was increased and I rejoiced in a new freedom in preaching; it became a joy instead of a burden. Preparation of sermons was looked at in a different light. Prayer became, not just a ritual, but a real, personal encounter with the living Lord.

Joy and peace flooded my soul as never before experienced; worry and tension took a back seat in my life. I do not mean I have never experienced tension or worry since then; I do mean I found freedom from these "bugaboos" that had played such a part in my ministry and life.

Another dimension of living came into being—life became a journey of expectancy rather than a burden of existence. I discovered that God wanted the very best of everything for his children, and that faith unlocks the door to the treasure of God's Kingdom. I discovered that positive living was part of positive believing and positive thinking. What one puts into the mind the mind reproduces.

It was some time before I shared what had taken place in my life. However one does not have to share verbally for people to know what has taken place in the inner man. I am sure the church realized they had a new preacher. The preacher knew he had found the secret to victorious living, believing, and proclaiming. Do not misunderstand what I am sharing. I still had problems, problems, problems, but the difference was my attitude toward them. I looked at the solutions, not the problems.

This great experience of the Holy Spirit made me realize that this was the problem with thousands of other Christians. They too were trying to do the work of God with the strength of man. Scriptures such as Luke 11:9-13 and John 7:37-39 began to have new meaning. The truth that Jesus wanted everyone to be filled with the Holy Spirit captivated my mind.

The first question that came to my mind was, "Why did I have to wait so long for this marvelous truth." Why didn't someone share with me that God wants to give strength, not take our strength? Why didn't someone share with me that to live in God's presence and power was as refreshing as the morning dew and delightful as the sunshine of a new day. That God wants from our lives a willingness to follow him with a sense of expectancy. Not to serve him from a sense of duty and dread. I like what I heard Ethel Waters say, "God don't sponsor no flops. He wants his children to be successful."

Following the complete turnover of my life to Christ I began to think differently concerning life. I discovered the way of gladness. The secret of trusting and believing. I was beginning to learn about God's great love for his sons and daughters. I began to rise in the morning with a desire to live and think creatively. Too long I had been hitchhiking on the brain power of other people. I had been willing to let others think for me.

Even during my college and seminary training it was easy to give the professor back what he gave to me in class.

A new day had broken forth in my life. No longer did I want to just get along the easy way—that is, without thinking. Rather, the Holy Spirit was teaching me that God wants everyone to be unusual. That is the reason he made each person unique. He expects each of us to be creative, to contribute something that no one else can contribute.

When the Holy Spirit becomes the teacher, ideas—big ideas, dreams—unusual dreams, vision—unlimited vision begin to invade the mind. I believe that the Holy Spirit can make anyone a possibility thinker, a creative person. The Holy Spirit knows nothing of negative thinking. He always believes it is possible, for with God all things are possible (Luke 1:37). The Bible says all things are possible for the believer (Mark 9:23).

With this new understanding of the power of the Holy Spirit, I began to develop a new philosophy of life. These ideas have been of unusual value in developing a great church.

God never calls a person to do anything unless He is willing to provide the resources to do the job. The church is God's work. He does not expect us to carry the burden—all he expects from us is the willingness to follow instructions. We do not have to worry and fret over the work if we are doing God's will. The God that created the whole universe can handle one situation if we will let him. I believe the reason why so many ministers are leaving the ministry is because they have forgotten who is to carry the burden.

Another titanic truth was taught me by the Holy Spirit. God is always bigger than our plans. The problem we have as ministers is seeing things *big*. God delights in helping us see big visions, dream big dreams, and attempt big, difficult tasks for his glory. The Bible says in Ephesians 3:20 that God is able to do more than we can think or ask through the power of God. John 14:12, "Verily, Verily I say unto you, he that believeth on me, the works that I do shall he do also; and greater works than these shall he do; because I go unto the Father."

The greatest step of wisdom in preparing for any great work in God's Kingdom is to first prepare the heart for the fullness of the Holy Spirit. God wants this for all of his children. No one can do the work of God without the power of God. An unconditional surrender of self is the only avenue to realizing the power of the Holy Spirit. One must be willing to turn his life over to Christ, if he wants the power of the Holy Spirit to energize him.

3
Prayers Are Answered

If Bus Number 5 were given the power of speech, it would have quite a story to tell. It would relate how it joined the fleet of buses at Graceland as one of the very first buses the church secured.

"Those early days were hard and difficult," it might say. "The folks in the church didn't know exactly how to make the bus ministry work as a genuine outreach effort." It would talk about the many Saturdays it didn't move at all from the bus barn, and how on the following morning it sometimes made the entire trip and returned to the church with very few people. Those were the days the bus workers learned to *pray* together before beginning the run on either Saturday or Sunday morning.

Bus Number 5, with a sneeze of gasoline or diesel fumes, would continue its story by telling of the days when the bus ministry became a genuine outreach arm of the church. In those days, not only did Bus Number 5 fill up, but all other buses did as well. The people had found the way. If Bus 5 could smile, it would have a grin from headlight to headlight. But there would be more.

Bus Number 5 grew older; it would not need to admit that—we could tell just by looking. And not too closely, either. The old bus might brag about the new motor which gave it life for many more miles. For a while it even thought it would continue to go on and on. It might blink a directional signal, calling attention to new tires put on both front and back somewhere along the way. When we look we discover something the old bus doesn't know; those tires are gone and the bus is standing still beside one of the doors of the church.

Bus 5 catches itself; it did know the tires were gone. But it seems happy over what has happened. "Yes," the old bus says. "When I was ready to be retired to my place behind the bus barn, the church needed a place for a prayer chapel. Hunt as the pastor and leaders might, they could discover no place not already in use for some activity. There was no place for a prayer chapel."

The bus would be right in saying that. The prayer ministry, so much a part of Graceland's life, needed a place. The ministry had been going on for years, but always without a home. The pastor and church staff wanted to challenge the people to a permanent round-the-clock prayer ministry. Some would pray at home, they knew, and others would come to one of the classes or assembly rooms. Yet, suppose someone wanted to pray at the church late at night or early in the morning and found the church closed.

So, today the bus that might have been retired is back on the church yard. It sits right up next to the building. Some of the men have taken its seats out, carpeted it, placed an easy chair or two inside, provided a table and a Bible. It has become a prayer chapel. Prayer volunteers and prayer warriors may come here to pray, as may anyone who wants to find a place where they can talk to the God who answers prayer.

At Graceland prayer is a definite and positive ministry of the church, organized and promoted as are the other church programs. At Graceland prayers are answered. Prayer is the heartbeat of the church. How did prayer come to be considered a ministry at Graceland?

"If ye have the faith as a grain of mustard seed, ye shall say unto this mountain, Remove hence to yonder place; and it shall be removed; and nothing shall be impossible to you" (Matt. 17:20).

The time had arrived to consider seriously the plan of advancement. I certainly believed that nothing was impossible with God. But I also believed that God had a plan for the advancement of his Kingdom. It was not my idea that Christ wanted us to go around saying to the mountain, "Be removed," and the terrain would become flat. I believe he was teaching that any problem which hinders the work of the Kingdom can be removed. I believe he was teaching that any barrier to happiness, joy, and peace can be overcome by faith. Nothing is impossible to the believer.

However, I know that Christ expects us to seek the guidance of the Holy Spirit, and if we will be obedient he will lead us step by step in accomplishing his purpose. The willingness to be obedient probably came the hardest for me. I am impatient by nature and only the work of the Holy Spirit could handle the problem.

To illustrate what I mean, let me use an experience I had during the last year of seminary. God was formulating his plan for advancement in my heart. I enrolled in Dr. Kenneth L. Chafin's class on "Evangelism in the Inner City." The first two or three weeks he assigned so many books that I became frustrated with the volumes he expected us to read.

I made an appointment with him. I went by his office to drop the class—I had no thought in mind other than to quit. I told Dr. Chafin I had so much to do in my ministry that it would be impossible for me to carry the study load. He convinced me to continue the course. The remarkable thing about the class was the preparation I gained for the ministry God had called me to direct. The class was a tremendous help to me. It was one of the most profitable in my seminary training in helping me develop a creative approach to ministering. I was taught that the task which often seems so difficult is not, if we take one step at a time.

The time had come to lead the church in the beginning stages of reaching a city for Jesus Christ. Months of preaching a positive gospel. Challenging the church to dream big dreams to dare to be different, and to dedicate their lives to living on the "cutting edge" of faith had brought us to this point. The laymen were beginning to ask, "When do we start reaching the city? When do we start ministering to the needy?"

As Benjamin Franklin once said, "It has been my experience in studying people that most people fail because they have no plan." I believe they know "why" is the first step to the know "how." Therefore, we began by developing a theological basis for a city-wide ministry.

THEOLOGICAL BASIS
FOR THE GRACELAND MINISTRY

1. Christ died for all men. Christ came to give life and to give it more abundantly. This meant that no man, woman, boy or girl was excluded from God's love. New Albany had thousands of people who had never been told about Christ's marvelous plan for abundant living. Therefore, we had to consider seriously the fact that a city-wide ministry would involve the church in ministering and loving the people *regardless of race, class, or living conditions.*

2. The gospel is a going thing. A further conviction was that Christ said, "Go." Too many churches have built buildings and beckoned for the people to come—they have waited for people to come. The people were not and are not coming to the buildings. Matthew 28:19-20 and Mark 16:15 are explicit orders to "Go." Jesus commanded: "Go out into the highways and hedges and compel them to come in, that my house may be filled" (Luke 14:23).

3. Ministry to the total man. A further theological basis for the Graceland ministry is that Christ sets the example for the church to follow in performing a Christian ministry to the "total man." Jesus was concerned and wants every Christian concerned about a person who is cold, hungry, naked, thirsty, lonely, in prison, sick, or with any other physical need he may have. The great text concerning this fact is found in Matthew 26:31-46. In verse 40, Jesus declared, "Inasmuch as ye have done it unto the least of these my brethren, ye have done it unto me."

I believe the gospel is concerned with the total man. It is

not segmented into social and spiritual aspects. The church has the responsibility to meet both physical and spiritual needs. James teaches that, "If a brother or sister is naked and destitute of daily food, and one of you say unto them Depart in peace, be ye warm and filled; notwithstanding ye give them not those things which are needful to the body: what doth it profit?" (James 2:15-16). The people were prepared through God's Word, prayer, and the Holy Spirit to look at the value of the individual to God—not to consider whether he was poor, black, or had plenty.

4. The purpose of the ministry. The Graceland ministry would be aimed at bringing persons to a saving faith in Jesus Christ. Leading them to discover that God had a plan for their lives. That God wants the best for all people. The love of Christ can change the lives of all, regardless of the past. Christ begins with us where we are and leads us to where he desires us to be.

We agreed that an evangelistic outreach would encompass the city. We would, through the love of Christ, attempt to meet each person at his greatest point of need and lead him to experience the marvelous love of Jesus Christ. "Neither is there salvation in any other for there is none other name (Jesus) under heaven given among men, whereby we must be saved" (Acts 4:12).

5. Every Christian a minister. We believe in the doctrine of the priesthood of the believer. Every Christian is a minister of Jesus Christ. The pastor is a leader and equipper of the congregation (Eph. 4:12). As a result of this concept our people are prepared to minister at work, at school, at home. Wherever there is a need God has a minister ready to meet that need. Our laymen are taught concerning their responsibility to share the work of ministering everywhere.

This concept has had tremendous influence in formulating the plans for a city-wide ministry and implementing those plans in progressive action. This is a logical approach to ministering. Laymen are more in number and have more money; they are where the action is. God ordained them to be ministers. Why not let them do God's will?

THE SECOND STEP:
DEVELOPING A PHILOSOPHY

Anyone who is going to accomplish much in life must first hammer out his philosophy. Likewise a church must develop a philosophy. The know "why" is the first step to the know "how."

The basic philosophy developed at Graceland is as follows:

1. God placed us here for "such a time as this."
2. The only thing that defeats us is our attitude. Our attitude can be our enemy or ally.
3. If we are doing what God wants done we have all the resources he has.
4. This is his work, not ours; he will carry the burden.
5. God placed us on earth to live victorious, creative lives, not to live in despair and defeat.
6. It is a marvelous day to be alive and minister for the Lord Jesus.
7. God is always bigger than our plans.
8. If we are concerned about a man going to hell, we are also concerned about his living in hell "now."
9. God calls us to minister to the total man.

This philosophy captured the hearts of the people and we were on our way to prepare for the "invasion" of a city.

In order to prepare for this spiritual invasion we began weeks and months of study on the following subjects:

1. The power of the Holy Spirit
2. How to be filled with the Holy Spirit
3. The fruits of the Holy Spirit
4. The work of the Holy Spirit

A study was made on the ministry of prayer. It included these aspects:

1. Involving the church in prayer
2. The power of prayer
3. Teaching members to pray
4. Developing a ministry of prayer

Out of this study came the development of a ministry of prayer which has had profound influence on the total ministry of the church. It has grown to involve many people who are committed daily to pray for each member in the fellowship by name. *Prayer Groups, Prayer Time, Prayer Retreat.*

Mrs. Connie Gettlefinger talks about her prayer experiences as a part of the church's prayer ministry and especially on the bus which has become the prayer chapel.

Mrs. Connie Gettlefinger: "As our church looked toward 'Miracle Week,' May 11 through 18, 1975, prayer seemed to become more needed and important to all of us. The prayer bus became a reality—a place to come and pray.

"I come to the bus now at my regular time. I read about the needs of other people, some who have themselves requested prayer and some for whom others have requested it. I think of the needs of these people and of their problems; then I pray for them one by one. Since learning to pray in this way, God has begun to use me. He has! My own troubles no longer seem so big, and opportunities for ministry seem to multiply. Through prayer, I have learned, God can reach out through me to help others."

Elizabeth Hollabaugh: "I had come to a point in my life where I felt I needed a High School diploma. I thought about it so much that I had developed a real inferiority complex about it. All my friends had a diploma and most of them had college degrees. I loved my job, but there was one problem—everyone at work had at least a high school diploma. This made my complex worse. One night as I was praying about this problem it seemed to me the Lord said, 'Well do something about it.' So I did.

"I started going to class every Monday night to study for the G.E.D. test, which is equal to a high school diploma. The only problem was Monday night was our visitation night for Sunday School. I tried to keep up with my work for the Lord and study, too. Seems like there just wasn't enough hours in the day to get things done. I worked a full-time job, tried to keep up with my visitation and all of my church work. Also, I have five children. I thought many times, 'I can do all things through Christ which strengtheneth me.'

"So, I studied and it seemed I didn't have any problem with anything but math. Oh, how I hate math. But, I studied and studied and several of my friends helped me until I had all of the basic math down pat. When it came to geometry I absolutely could not understand it, and I still can't.

"The test came in five parts. I took the first four parts, English, literature, history and science. It seemed I did all right on these subjects. Then it came to the last test, MATH.

"Before I went to take the test I prayed and prayed for the Lord to help me. When I got to the school and took one look at the math I felt like crying. There were fifty questions of solid geometry. I knew how to do *one problem*. Well, I sat there and looked at it for a few minutes—then I just started praying. I told the Lord I didn't know how to do any of these problems and he was going to have to take over. I had studied and studied for this test, and here I was, and I didn't know how to do any of the math at all. So it would all have to be up to Him. So, on each problem (there were fifty multiple-choice) I prayed for God to show me which one to mark down. When I finished the test I went home confident the Lord had taken care of it. I hadn't been home 15 minutes before the devil started picking on me. He said, 'You big dummy, you didn't pass that test—you failed. God can't be bothered with things like that.' But God gave me assurance.

"It took a week to find out the score. I was sure that I passed, but there was that little doubt. Well, the day finally came and they called me at work to tell me I had passed, and that I could pick up my score anytime. I sent my daughter to get my test score. She called me back at work to tell me the score. They give you your score and then they give you the percent for the United States.

"On each subject I made a score maybe two or three points lower than the percent for the United States. Then my daughter gave me my math score. I made 44% and the percent for the United States is 27%. I said, 'Now, wait, you've got that backwards. 'I couldn't have made a higher score than the rest of the United States.'

"I started crying and I went into my bedroom and got down on my knees and thanked God and praised him. I knew he had helped me put those answers down. Later I called my teacher and asked him if a mistake had been made. He told me he was sure that it was right. Not only that, but I had made the second highest score on these.

"Then came the problem of how to share this with other people. If they could only depend on God for everything. I was afraid if I shared it at prayer meeting people would think I was bragging. So I just shared it with a few of my closest friends.

"Then I got sick and had to go to the hospital and the pastor came to see me and I told him about it. He used it in his sermon Sunday morning. I was glad that maybe by hearing this even one person may learn to depend on God for everything."

There it is. For Graceland prayer is a planned way of ministering to the needs of fellow church members and to those outside the church fellowship. Yes, it's made a miraculous difference.

Organizing a Prayer Ministry

An organized, positively-functioning prayer ministry will be one of the most vital and helpful ministries of any church. Christ, our Lord, is the foundation stone of a church and the rock upon which the life of the individual Christian stands. But prayer is the medium through which the Christian, and through which a church, enjoys constant fellowship and touch with the living Lord.

For a church, continuing prayer brings down the presence of God and his abundant power through the Holy Spirit. Jesus promised that his disciples, his witnesses, would do greater things than he himself; through prayer this promise, and indeed all the promises Christ made to his people, are realized.

Since all of the foregoing is true, a prayer ministry seems natural for a church. Why should a church not involve in prayer all its willing members? Why should it not organize its ministry so it will be directed toward all the objects of the church program and all the people for whom the church feels a spiritual responsibility?

The first New Testament church had such a program of prayer. It continued—at least in the early days—hour after hour through the day and through the night. If a church today desires such a ministry, however, it must plan for it and the church leaders must guide the church in putting it into effect. How can a church go about this?

1. Prepare the church.

Teach the value of prayer. Use the Wednesday evening prayer service and all other appropriate occasions to do this. Deal with the value of prayer for the individual Christian. Show what prayer does for a church. Lead church members to realize what happens when a church becomes a praying church. Use every possible opportunity to impress this upon the people.

Share answers to prayer. Prayer answers should be shared; each one is a victory for God's people. How can this be done? Set aside a sharing time in the services each week. Wednesday night is a good time, or it may be done at Sunday evening services. Many smaller meetings, such as planning meetings, may use a part of the time for sharing prayer victories. Sharing in this manner is good, not only for preparing a church to enter upon a definite prayer ministry, but also after the ministry has been initiated. It should become a part of the life-style of the church.

Impart an understanding of being filled with the Holy Spirit. A praying church and a Spirit-filled church are synonymous. A praying church becomes a Spirit-filled church. If the church can be led to "pray unceasingly," the Holy Spirit will bless with his presence and power (Luke 11:9-13).

Emphasize the relationship between prayer and outreach. This is a direct and positive relationship. Prayer produces concern and concern inevitably leads to performance of spiritual ministries. A church that prays will look inward toward the needs of its fellowship; it will also look outward to the spiritual need of the vast multitudes of people all around. The outward look of concern soon becomes more; it becomes an outreach ministry. The fruit of a prayer ministry is outreach.

Challenge the people to a program of prayer. Share with them your vision of a church that prays, not merely in the usual way as an almost perfunctory part of the worship services, but as a definite, specific, and continuing ministry.

2. Ask for volunteers.

Present the ministry as having as definite and specific a place in the church organization as a teacher or leader. The function is as important as any other in the church, if not more so. The commitment to it is also definite, and carries the same responsibility to be faithful in performance. Ask for volunteers for the ministry. Prepare cards and have them available so that those who volunteer may be recorded.

3. Prepare prayer responsibility lists.

Each of the prayer responsibility lists should contain (1) a committed family, (2) an uncommitted family, and (3) a prospect for salvation. The prospect for salvation could be related in some way to the church family, such as husband, wife, or child of a church member. However, the prospect may be a part of a family, some of whose members are enrolled in Bible study, or may be someone as yet untouched by the church.

4. Assign prayer responsibility.

Every person who volunteers for service will be assigned a list as his responsibility. At some time during every day he prays for those on his list.

5. Keep records of the work.

Include in the record both the names of those who are participating in the ministry and the lists of those persons for whom prayer is being offered each day. The responsibility of keeping these records may be assigned to a church staff member or may be given to a lay person in the church. The records should be a part of the church record system.

6. Reassign responsibility quarterly.

Each quarter new responsibility lists should be distributed. New prayer volunteers may be included for assignments. Some families which were uncommitted to the church program may now be assigned as committed families. Some prospects will have become members of the church and new prospects may have been discovered and added to the prayer responsibility list. The new assignments should be given by mail.

7. Organize special prayer groups.

Various prayer groups may meet regularly throughout the week. Groups of men may meet for prayer. Groups of women also may organize and meet for prayer. These may be in addition to the individual prayer responsibility.

8. Continue emphasis on the prayer ministry.

Such a continuing emphasis on the place of prayer in ministering is necessary to keep the people aware of their responsibility. This emphasis should be a part of the pastor's leadership role.

9. Use the prayer groups and prayer volunteers for special prayer.

When major events are scheduled for the life of the church, or when the church faces major decisions as to the direction of its program, the prayer volunteers and the prayer groups may be asked to pray. They may pray for God's guidance and the Holy Spirit's power upon the church as it seeks to honor and glorify Christ.

Hundreds of testimonies concerning Graceland's prayer ministry could be given. Here is one.

Bill Newman: "For a long time as a Christian I was lukewarm and my Christianity had no real relationship to my everyday living. But one day Jesus became Lord in my life and from that moment on every aspect of my life radically changed. This was true of my thoughts, my actions, my attitudes, and my emotions. Everything about me changed.

"I think about the many ways that God has been able to work through me especially in regard to prayer. I think about how I've seen God answer prayer and how I've been able to work through outreach. How I've been able to get down on my knees and pray with a person who needed Jesus. How I've gone to a hospital to visit a person and when I'd get there that person would be gone, but I would find another who had been praying for someone to come and talk to him about Jesus—through all of this God was leading. This has all happened since Jesus became Lord of all my life. Before, I was never to talk about him on the job or to witness for him, but since he has been Lord I have been able to do this, and he has given me real excitement in my Christian living."

4
Lay People Are Involved

"I am just a layman," is heard half-apologetically from the lips of laymen, as if to say, not much expected, not much attempted. What's wrong with being a layman? Nothing is wrong with being a layman at Graceland Baptist Church—in fact, laymen are ministers to needs. They have invaded the city with enthusiasm, excitement, and creative ideas.

"Watch out, he's a layman at our church" means: here is a person who has found the secret of abundant living. No longer is he content to sit in the pew and listen to the preacher proclaim the good news. He wants part of the action. He has experienced the joy of dedicated service. He is ready to share the miraculous work of the Holy Spirit. He has come to believe that all things are possible for the believer, that prayer unlocks the treasuries of heaven. He has a key to the Kingdom of God's blessing. No longer does he believe the preacher should experience all the joy of discovering a new approach to reaching the hearts of people. He wants to be part of the outreach. He enjoys the "happenings" that take place with God when a person walks moment by moment in his Spirit.

One of our laymen taught me a great lesson. One afternoon as we were traveling together, we passed three young men who were hitchhiking. I must admit my faith is a little weak at this point, due to the experience of a minister friend of mine from college days. He had picked up a fellow whom he did not know. Later, in an old barn they found the young minister with a bullet in the back of his head. When they caught the killer there was no real motive for the killing. Therefore, the incident with one of my laymen had a greater significance because he chose to do something I was apprehensive about doing. Another reason for the profound impression was the fact that he was a company executive and did not make it a habit of picking up hitchhikers.

As we passed the fellows he began to slow down his station wagon. He asked me if I thought we should give them a ride. I replied with a lot of stuttering and stammering and really said nothing. By this time he had turned around, and was on his way back to give them a lift.

The young men got into the station wagon. Just a few miles down the road we found that they were seminary students from a Catholic seminary in another state.

The tremendous truth that came out of this incident was the statement the layman made when he said, "I believe that the Holy Spirit leads a person moment by moment, not just day by day. I believe that God told me to pick up those hitchhikers." The idea of living "moment by moment in his Spirit" has become a living reality in my life.

We were beginning to see a revolution take place in the minds and hearts of the laymen. Their lives had been challenged by an amazing dream. They believed that God had placed them here for "such a time as this." They believed in a positive approach to living, that it is a good day to be alive, and God is going to do something special today.

To share the spirit that was captivating the minds of the laymen, I want you to meet one of the miracle men of the mighty movement of God's Holy Spirit. Ed McCrary is a man in his early forties. He was born in Alabama and moved to New Albany when he was a young adult. Ed became a Christian about the year 1959. Up to this time the church had not impressed him much.

Ed did not have the privilege of much formal training. However, the spirit of the church and the power of the Holy Spirit began to motivate Ed to use his talents and time for Jesus Christ. He owned an engine rebuilding company and was a master mechanic. But little did he realize what a tremendous challenge

God was going to present to him. He had his mind and heart filled with positive expectancy. He knew the only thing that defeated a person was his attitude. He believed in the unlimited power of the Holy Spirit.

Ed started developing a bus ministry long before Southern Baptists ever dreamed of buses being used as widely as they are now. He was a mechanic motivator, and often called "agitator" to get more buses. He has helped build one of the largest bus ministries in the Southern Baptist Convention. But not only did he help build a great bus ministry at Graceland Baptist Church, he has helped a large number of other people locate buses, buy buses, and build a bus ministry. At the last count Ed had helped somewhere around 50 to 60 churches start bus ministries. This does not include the many others he has talked to about the ministry and those he has helped with counsel.

Ed McCrary has more calls from across America asking for advice and help than most ministers. This was just the beginning for a layman who practiced positive believing.

Another great experience took place in his life. The Regional Vocational School in Floyd County needed a teacher to head up the mechanical department. The superintendent of the Floyd County school system called Ed to come to his office for an interview. Ed went at the appointed time, and was asked to step into the office.

The superintendent began to talk to Ed about this position. Ed told him that he had no high school and no college, and that he didn't know if they would have any interest in him after realizing his lack of formal training. They discussed the position a little longer and then Ed went home. A few days later he was called back to the school office. They had decided to give him a high school diploma for four years' experience, pay equal to a college degree for four more years of experience, pay equal to a master's degree for four more years of experience, and he still had enough experience for a doctor's degree. We don't know when that will be awarded!

Ed still had one other problem to work out. He was not willing to give up his speaking and his work for the Lord. He told them he put Christ first in everything. There would be times he would have to be away. This was worked out to his satisfaction, and he was given the position as head of the department.

God continues to use Ed in an unusual manner. He was used to influence two teachers to seek Jesus Christ as Savior and Lord. I had the privilege of baptizing the entire family of five people. Ed led the other teacher in his department to accept Christ. I have baptized him and he is active in the ministry.

The other day Ed was called into the office to talk with the superintendent of the school system and fourteen school principals from the surrounding counties about providing transportation for handicapped children to Indianapolis each week. They will use the "Tour Bus," a non-profit, cross-country tour bus service our men have organized as a ministry of the Graceland Baptist Church.

These true stories illustrate how God uses men and women who are positive thinkers to do remarkable things in God's service.

One of our laymen was used as the key to reaching the high-rise complex in our city. One of the older ladies had suffered a loss of one member of the family. The layman heard about it, made a visit and through this contact the entire high-rise complex for older people was open to our ministry.

Another one of our laymen, a businessman from Atlanta, Georgia, has been the minister to the high-rise. One day a group from the high-rise went on a bus trip, and they passed by his place of business. They stopped and he came out to greet them. A newcomer in the group asked who the man was. One of the ladies who had been in his Sunday School class, but is a Catholic, said, "He is our priest!" Yes, he truly is a priest of the high calling of Jesus Christ. His love for the people has been the reason for many miraculous happenings. One lady goes to early Mass, so she will not miss his Sunday School class in the high-rise building. Hundreds of people have been touched and changed by this ministry.

One of our laymen came up with the idea of a "mini-church." On Sunday morning he goes out into the city and visits those that cannot go to church. He has a short Scripture lesson and prayer with the person or persons and then moves to another location for another mini-church.

The spirit of the layman must be felt, as well as shared, to really get the full impact of the movement.

A sociology teacher from the University of Louisville was teaching a course over at Indiana University Extension Campus in Jeffersonville, Indiana. One of our staff members was taking the course. During the class one day he had the privilege of sharing the outreach ministry of Graceland.

The teacher responded by saying that she did not believe there was a church anywhere doing what he claimed Graceland was doing. He invited her to come and see. Little did we expect what followed. She and her husband drove from the east side of Louisville, where they lived, to attend one of our services. They were members of a Christian Church, and she had never been affiliated with a Baptist church. The week after they attended the morning worship service, she wrote a letter of appreciation and sent a check as a donation.

What was to come out of that visit was later seen. This showed the tremendous spirit of the people. Several months had passed and a phone call came from the professor. She asked if it would be all right to bring 35 Japanese people to church, who were visiting from their native land. Many of the students had never attended an American worship service. The professor remarked, "I could have chosen my church or several others, but I wanted to bring them to Graceland." Needless to say we were thrilled at the opportunity. The day they arrived at the service the professor said, "I don't think they will understand much of what goes on in the service, but I believe they will feel the spirit of worship."

A lay person was really the motivation behind the prayer ministry that has had such a profound and far-reaching effect on our church and many others. Another denomination is using our prayer ministry as a model. Many churches have used the prayer ministry effectively.

I want you to meet Miss Clara Meyers. It is said, "When Miss Clara prays things happen." Miss Meyers spent her life in city mission work. She is one of the most radiant Christians that I have met. I personally have requested prayer from her in times of need. She has lived by faith, and her life is a pattern of what Christ-like living does for a person. Long before the church had reached the spiritual maturity to know the value of prayer, Miss Clara was trying to organize prayer groups. She personally recognized the power of communicating with God. Daily she prayed for the church and her pastor. Out of this knowledge that someone was daily praying for me and an idea from Dr. Shedd's book, *A Praying Church,* came the formulation of a prayer ministry where every member and Sunday School member are prayed for by name daily. Miracle after miracle has come forth from this ministry. The outline of how to develop a praying church is presented in the previous chapter.

The transforming power of Jesus is in the worship, weekday work, and the witness of the layman. The laymen are discovering that they can make a notable contribution to life. Living is more than day by day existence; it is a moment-by-moment walk in His presence. More and more laymen are challenged to think, act, and expect something unusual to happen. One layman who has traveled around the world said, "The thing I like about Graceland is the fact one never knows what exciting thing is going to happen next." This is always true when God has the freedom to work in the lives of lay persons.

A layman who worked in the real estate business began to use much of his time helping the needy buy homes, thereby changing their environment, as well as their spiritual lives. He spent hundreds of hours working on projects of help for the people who had never dreamed it would be possible for them to own a house or to move from the "caste system" they seemed destined to live in the remainder of their lives.

I cannot forget one case this layman worked on several months, and it is doubtful that he broke even on the expense. Nevertheless, the day he heard about the appraisal for the loan, as he spoke to me on the phone, he was almost like a little child that had just greeted Santa Claus. He was as thrilled for the family as one would have been for his own home.

The love of Christ is contagious. No one climbs the ladder of noble achievement without each step being motivated by love. The love of Christ is touching lives across the city. Men and women are sharing their faith in an intelligent way. One man was asked why he smiled so much as he was servicing a customer's car. He replied, "It is my church, and my Lord." The customer said, "If your church will do that for you, where is it?" He told the customer about Graceland. She attended and I had the privilege of baptizing her and her two daughters.

The same man I just mentioned had spent his entire life in the community without giving much thought to Jesus Christ. One day he and his family, more from curiosity than any other reason, came to visit the fellowship. They were members on record of another denomination. In the following weeks, not only his family, but his father and stepmother, became part of the fellowship.

Only a few months later he became part of the contagious love of Christ and began to experience the overwhelming joy of commitment to Christ. He and a group of young people provided Sunday services for two rest homes. Each morning for a week he arose early to visit one of these homes and exercise an old gentleman who needed help in learning to walk again. In appreciation for the wonderful service rendered, the people of rest homes provided a food feast out on the sidewalk for members of the church, along with the people of the home.

In the midst of the spiritual growth of the laymen, the need for another staff member to share the work at home base was felt. After months of prayer and searching for a man to fill the gap, Rev. Jeff Barbour and his wife, Kay, were chosen. Jeff was already in the mission work. He had been director of the Bono Mission, the Green Valley area, and now had the opportunity to become part of the inner staff. Jeff was destined to play a pivotal part in the development of "Junior Church," the outreach program, and bus ministry. Along with his wife, Kay, he developed the school. He, like the rest of the staff, was privileged to work with a large group of laymen who were always coming up with a new approach to ministry.

One day the word came to the office that a new addition had been made to the staff without the vote or selection of the church. One of the laymen had bought one pony and had been given two more. Immediately the church was confronted with the naming and ordaining of the ponies for ministry!

Some suggested that we name them Jeremiah, Isaiah, or Ezekiel but the laymen decided they would name them after the pastor's family. Therefore, they were named Elvis, Virginia, and Alan. No doubt the next would be named Steve.

The ponies were used in the park, parades, Bible School, and in housing projects. Everything went well until one day the word came ringing into the office that Elvis had gotten loose and was running wild! After a chase he was captured and everything was back to normal.

Our laymen are always specializing in the unusual. In the middle of a busy schedule, one of the fellows called. He wanted to see me about "something that was very important." I wondered what was up now. He dropped by the office and shared it with me. He and another layman had found a need in their ministry.

A young couple that they had been working with wanted to get married. The parents had no concern for either of the young people. The laymen had decided to provide a church wedding for the couple. They enlisted me and the services of the organist and minister of music. They talked to both sets of parents, which were divorced, and the mothers on both sides agreed to attend. The laymen paid for a room at the Holiday Inn for the honeymoon. On the day of the wedding the laymen who had planned their first wedding were as happy as a mother who had provided a magnificent wedding for her oldest daughter. The laymen led this young couple to make their decisions for Christ.

Our deacons are men who are willing to go the second mile in service and love. They believe that it is an honor from the church and a blessing from God to be chosen to fill this place of responsibility. However, I want to share the attitude of one that expresses the feeling of all. He is noted for his compassionate heart for people and his warm devotion to Jesus Christ. He has optimism and is always more than willing to give of his time, talent, and material blessings. He's a great man of prayer.

He believes that whatever is needed, God will supply. Through planning and prayer we came to feel the need for a half-million dollars to further our ministry. This deacon challenged all the deacons and staff to make this a matter of prayer, believing that God will provide. This deacon is noted for his tireless efforts from day to day. His explanation is that the Holy Spirit is his strength and help. He said, "I used to stay tired and negative most of the time, but since I have discovered the power of the Holy Spirit I have this strength."

Involving Lay People

How can a church involve its lay people in the church program? A good answer can be found in the title of a Convention Press book, written by Frank Foutch and Eugene Skelton. It relates the story of the First Baptist Church of Houston, Texas. What is the title? *Involving People in Reaching People.* Some specifics—not necessarily all, but some—may be given.

1. Challenge them with a big dream.

Such a dream of great and mighty deeds to be done for the Lord's glory will lift people out of petty things, turn their thoughts away from themselves, and give them a direction in Christian living.

2. Show them confidence and enthusiasm.

Lay people have enough frustrations and fears on their own; they need from their pastor and church staff a feeling of confidence, enthusiasm, and joy. They catch the spirit of their leaders; give them the best.

3. Trust them to do their best.

Sometimes lay people fail because they are not trusted by their leaders to perform the tasks of the church. If the pastor places complete trust in his lay people, they will respond.

4. Lead in an exciting program.

Lay people are used to doing big things in the workaday world. They can do the same in their church life. Lay people may not respond to petty quarrels and quibbling; they will rise to the occasion when challenged to reach a city for Christ.

5
Buses Go Out

On a Sunday in October, 1972, bus pastor (bus captain) Reubin Seese swung open the door of his big black-and-white bus and stepped off to the ground at the door of Graceland. Sixty-three people followed, small children, youth, and some adults. Reubin smiled as he greeted each by name, wished him a joyous experience in Bible study, and reminded him the bus would be waiting at a later hour for the return trip home.

As he watched the last person disappear into the church building and then stepped into the bus, motioning the driver to move into the assigned parking space, he thought what a joy it was to drive through a neighborhood, pick up sixty-three people, and transport them to church. He remembered the first time he'd gone out with a bus. That was some eight months earlier.

The bus route really began on the day when Reubin felt that God had called him to the bus outreach ministry—and made a commitment to follow God's leadership. He was assigned a bus and an area to work. He received instruction from the bus director, listening carefully and trying to understand. He attended several Saturday morning bus meetings, in the meantime enlisting four or five people to help knock on doors in his area. After all was ready, the Saturday he was to begin came. February 27, 1972.

He and his workers went into the four-block wide, fifteen-block long area where they were to make their search for people to whom they could minister. The housing ranged from old mansions to apartments renting for only $20 a week. After working for several hours, Reubin called his workers together to assess what they'd done. Some had listened with no response, some had replied they were already enrolled in Bible study somewhere and attended each Lord's Day, some had listened and made no reply at all. But some had answered yes, they'd like to ride a bus to Bible study at Graceland.

Not everyone who indicated an interest rode that first Sunday morning. But thirteen people did ride. Reubin was encouraged. The following week he carried his wife with him to make calls. The two of them, with big smiles on their faces, visited every person who'd ridden to Graceland the previous Sunday. They also visited every person who'd shown any interest at all the previous Saturday. Then they began working for new riders.

Many times that day Reubin's hand went into his pocket and came out with a candy treat, an enticement to create a more ready response. But he knew the real treat was for those who would ride the bus the next morning. Nineteen people did ride that day, Reubin's second Sunday as bus pastor.

Reubin soon discovered there was more to starting and growing a bus route than merely driving through the city. Or even making the necessary visits. He found that the people on his route needed someone to love them; he learned also that if he loved them, they loved him in return, and it was no trouble— no trouble at all—to fill his bus. Reubin and his wife gave that love, and soon the people filled his bus.

During the first eight months, 231 new people rode his bus for the first time. Forty-nine regular riders moved away; sixty-seven attended irregularly. But 115 attended Sunday by Sunday. Reubin's bus goes out; it returns with from sixty to one hundred people each Sunday morning. Those who ride Reubin's bus call him "Pastor Reubin." How would Reubin speak of his work?

Reubin Seese: "My wife and I have used many promotional ideas to help get people to ride our bus to Graceland. We always give a small treat of some kind to any one who brings a friend with him. Once we spent two dollars for 100 "Smile, God Loves You" pressure sensitive stickers. We stuck one on each child as he got on the bus. Adults, too—those who were willing. I wore one. That Sunday almost every child in Sunday School wanted to ride home on our bus.

"The church gave new Bibles to the children who came ten Sundays in a row. At the end of that effort I gave Bibles to twenty-four additional children who never before had owned Bibles of their own. My wife and I paid for those.

"We decided to have a picnic in the park for our riders and began promoting that a month in advance of the date we chose. It was not to get people to ride our bus, but because we wanted to do something for those who already were riding. We had seventy-nine riders the Sunday before and had seventy-nine at the picnic. We served hot dogs and pop, gave out cotton candy, played games, and in general gave every one the chance to have a good time. This cost my wife and me about fifty dollars; we received that much joy from doing it. Another time we took our people to the zoo, spending another twenty-five dollars.

"You may think from all this that spending money is the way to get people to ride your bus. Nothing could be farther from the truth; if anyone tried to build a bus route with just money, he would be in for a big surprise. You must spend the time to visit the people week by week in their homes, and further, you must be willing to share yourself with them.

"Stanley is one boy I think of. He was about five years old when we first enlisted him to ride our bus. He never seemed to get along with anyone. Not that he was very much trouble; he just sat around and did not warm up to any one. But one Sunday he hopped off the bus and walked away—then he turned around and came back to give me a big kiss on the cheek. He knew I cared and that I was sharing my life with him. Not that he could have put his feelings into words. But he didn't need to.

"Many of those who ride our bus have accepted Christ as Lord and Savior. Others who were inactive or who had left their church membership back in some old home place have come into Graceland and have become active in the Lord's service. One Sunday ten people from our bus walked the aisle of our church. Two teenagers who began riding our bus at the very first are now bus workers themselves. We reached out to them, and now they are reaching out to still others who need to know Jesus.

"When I was up to be elected a deacon, some of the adults on the bus asked my wife what I would do if elected. 'Will he continue to work on this bus?' they asked. 'Yes,' my wife replied. 'Nothing will cause him to stop riding this bus.' 'Then we'll vote for him for deacon,' they replied. My wife spoke for both of us. We serve the Lord at Graceland through the bus outreach ministry. It gives us happiness and joy to see how God uses what we do to reach more people."

Our bus captain, John Baker, brings about 100 people a week to the services. He captains not one, but two buses, quite a job, when the Saturday visitation is taken into consideration. He is himself a product of the bus ministry of the church and laughs as he gives credit to the bus outreach program for finding first his children, then his wife, and finally himself. Although reared in a Christian home and saved when young, he had been a backslidden Christian for more than fifteen years. Then the church found him.

John Baker: "Clarence Rogers started coming by my house and picking up my boy, Jackie. Often, when he came by I'd be polishing my boat or something like that, maybe drinking a beer, although I don't think Clarence ever caught me doing anything like that. He did find me working on my boat, however. He'd ask me if it was all right for Jackie to go to church and I'd tell him whatever the boy wanted to do. I wasn't going to make him go; he could go on if he wanted to.

"But Jackie kept on going and I think that was one of the things that brought me back to the church. I always look back on that and on another thing. My little boy started going to kindergarten at the church, and later on Kay Barbour came by the house with someone else from the church. She asked me if I had a personal relationship with Jesus. I knew I was saved, but was not close to the Lord. What she asked me touched my heart and I didn't forget it.

"Later on my wife started going to church. She got mixed up with some Christians there and that was good for me. Sometimes a wife will hop on her husband, sort of nag him, and I guess you can't blame her, but my wife surprised me. She didn't do that. I couldn't figure out what was going on. She seemed to love me more, and I knew something was happening. Then some of the women in her group began to pray for me and I think their prayers are what made the difference.

"You know, it's harder for some people to come back to church than it is for others. I was one of the harder ones. But I came back. I was something like the lost sheep which came back to the fold. That day I remember I came to the front and got down on my knees and Brother Marcum prayed with me. He asked me if I would follow Christ if he showed me what he wanted me to do.

"I said I would and I prayed for guidance. I had my joy again. Soon I was asked to work on a bus and I have been a bus captain ever since. I'm glad the bus workers didn't stop, and the kindergarten workers were concerned for, and the women prayed for, me. I praise the Lord for what he has done for me."

A bus ministry offers a most rewarding way to present the love of Christ. However, if it is to be true to its purpose, it must include much more than just a "hauling to the church ministry." We use our buses as rolling chapels and Sunday School classes. We provide ministries to schools, clubs, and other organizations. Wherever there are needs our buses can meet, we are committed to meeting those needs through Jesus Christ our Lord. An effective bus ministry demands dedication and work from the pastor and the laymen. The church must be convinced of the value of the ministry and committed to the work involved. As with all other ministries, the ministry must be undergirded by the ministry of prayer.

The following steps are essential in developing a bus ministry:

1. Locate the needy places and the needs that can be met through the bus ministry. List all the possibilities that you can think about related to a bus ministry. Survey the location.
2. Vote on organizing a bus ministry through the regular business meeting. Share with the people the needs that can be met through this ministry.
3. Prayerfully select leadership that is committed to mission outreach and hard work. Select bus drivers (at least two per bus), bus captains, (men, women, or young people) and visitation helpers.
4. Make up a prospect list from the location.
5. Locate a bus—we have buses that have been used by the city transit company, the school corporation, the mail service (post office buses) and regular station wagons.

Contrary to popular opinion, and based on several years' experience, one should not invest a large sum in purchasing a vehicle. An average should be $600 to $1,000. Our buses will not average this much excluding the cross-country buses we use for long trips.

Use the men of the church in painting and maintaining the buses if possible. This creates a splendid missionary spirit in the church and cuts the operating expense. Insurance and license are inexpensive items. License cost, in the State of Indiana, is $16 per bus. Gas per week will run from around $10 to $13 depending on the route. The insurance runs about $50 per bus per year.

The bus ministry is invaluable in reaching all ages of people, publicizing the ministry of the church and making the community aware that you care.

Launching the Program

Some churches have thought all they needed to do was to buy buses, paint the church name on them, run them up and down the streets, and watch their Sunday School attendance zoom upward, as if by some kind of magic. Neither a bus program nor outreach of any kind works that way.

Reaching people is not an impersonal thing; it requires much time given in caring and sharing. Churches which think money and equipment bring success soon become disappointed and disillusioned and park their buses on the front lawn of the church with a large "For Sale" sign written across their windshields. What can a church do to launch a successful program of bus outreach? Graceland found the following guidelines helpful.

1. *Be flexible.* As the number of children and adults being reached grows larger, you will find places where you ought to make changes. In Graceland, the church began with all children attending the regular Sunday School and worship service. Soon space became a problem. Other problems also surfaced themselves. A children's worship service seemed necessary and was launched.

Then the space could not be stretched any further and a part of the Sunday School—the Youth Division—was moved to a nearby junior high school. The vision enlarged and parts of the Sunday School began meeting in other places. Had the program been inflexible, our people unwilling to change and adjust, reaching people would have reached its limit within a short period of time. As it is, the program has not begun to reach its limit. No one really knows how much farther we can go.

2. *Enlist workers.* This must be a constant, never-ending effort. The number of workers you can enlist and train—while maintaining a solid base of adults in the church—will be about the only real limitation you face. Space can be used more than once on Sunday morning. Schedules can be adjusted, and additional buses can be purchased.

With these adjustments made, a greater number of people can be reached. But without a sufficient number of workers, your bus outreach ministry cannot continue to grow. Workers are needed for the buses, for the Sunday School classes and departments, for the children's worship services, for the support activities such as preparing Saturday morning meals and Sunday morning snacks for the workers, and for other activities connected with bus outreach. Even when you seem to have enough workers, you ought to be enlisting new ones. They will make it possible for you to maintain your program and enlarge it as the Lord leads.

3. *Use good methods.* This does not mean that vigorous promotion, what some would classify as "gimmickry," is out of place. No, this will help reach more people. But they will not keep coming unless they receive something when they come. So use the very best educational methods and approaches. Use the best literature. Train the teachers and leaders to become excellent Bible teachers. Lead them to show concern, along with their use of the very best methods. The Lord will give the increase.

4. *Keep the church informed.* Work at keeping a good image of the bus outreach program before the people. Inform them about what is being done and let them see what is being accomplished. An informed church is a church that supports the program. Time spent on good public relations is time well spent.

5. *Aim for entire families.* The work of the bus ministry is not complete when the children of a family are reached. Go out after the adults. Many bus workers at Graceland were themselves reached for the church because some bus captain enlisted their children and then refused to give up. Every child comes from a home of some kind, a home where there are adults. These adults have a spiritual hunger which your church can meet.

6. *Solve problems quickly.* The creation of a bad image results from children running wild all over the church buildings. If this condition occurs, act quickly before you lose the entire bus program. Other problems can be just as disastrous in their effects. The sooner you face each problem, arrive at a possible solution, and then do something about it, the better off you and your program will be.

7. *Show appreciation.* Serving in a bus ministry is hard; the church has no position or place of service that demands more in commitment and downright hard work. Often a half-hearted

church member finds new fulfillment as a Christian through participation in the bus ministry, even though it demands much of his time. The demands it makes are in part responsible for the personal satisfaction it brings. It is also a good idea to express over and over again the appreciation of the church and its leaders for good work done well and faithfully.

Enlisting Workers

The key to success in the bus outreach ministry is not the number of buses in operation. The key is the dedication of the committed people who make up the bus teams. The bus workers are the ones who go from door to door on Saturdays, visiting and enlisting boys and girls, men and women to attend and become a part of regular, ongoing Bible study. The bus is the tool they use to give a better and clearer expression of care and concern. Reduced to its simplest terms, the bus ministry is *people going after people.* If workers are indeed the key, included in the list of workers should be all those who teach and work in the classes, the departments, and the worship services, as well as those who actually work on the buses. The following guidelines apply most specifically to the bus workers but also are applicable to all these others.

1. *Let the pastor take leadership.* People respond to the pastor and his leadership. If he shows that the program is his, they will respond. They see whether he attends the Saturday visitation. Even if he comes only for the breakfast and the prayer service and does not go out with the actual visitation, they are aware that he is supporting the program. The people know when the pastor comes for the Sunday morning bus departure time; they also know when he fails to show an interest in the program. Anything the pastor supports has a good chance of succeeding in the church—anything ignored or shoved aside by the pastor usually fails. Of all church programs, the bus program must have pastoral support, guidance, and direction the most.

2. *Give pulpit support to the program.* In the same vein, the

pastor can support the bus program from his pulpit. From this vantage he can motivate his people about the work and the benefits of the program and can appeal to them for support.

3. *Make public appeals for workers.* Opportunities to surrender to the Lord's leadership should be offered frequently, if not at every service. If this is done, people will volunteer for service, not always to the bus ministry, but for various ministries of the church. Individual counseling and guidance can lead a person to discover where Christ wants to use him in the church. Public decisions for rededication often will be accompanied by an expressed willingness to accept a place of service.

4. *Enlist people individually.* Even those who volunteer publicly should be enlisted individually for specific tasks. Others likewise should be enlisted individually. At times bus leaders will be impressed to speak to a person. The prospective worker may be a new member of the church or perhaps one who has been in the membership for some time, but has not been enlisted for a place of service. A good plan is to maintain a list of prospective workers and from this list find those who may be enlisted for service on one of the bus routes, or in some other area of service related to the bus program.

5. *Conduct regular training meetings.* These meetings may be conducted on Wednesday evenings as a part of the regular workers' council meeting. They may be conducted during the Church Training hour on Sunday evening. Special periods of training for bus personnel may be conducted from time to time. The church may make possible attendance of workers at bus clinics, conducted by individual churches or by denominational leadership. Training should always be a part of the Saturday morning meetings preparatory to going out for visitation. Individual training on a one-to-one basis is also effective. A well trained worker does a better job.

Outline to prospective workers what the church will do to provide training for them. Many or most of these prospective workers will never have served in a bus ministry before. They will wonder how to do the job. Offering training at the time of enlistment will make it easier for the worker to begin.

People in the church who might be interested in working with the program will know of the training offered and may find it easier to volunteer or respond to appeals for service.

6. *Bathe enlistment in prayer.* "Pray the Lord of the harvest that he will send forth labourers into his harvest." Every ministry of the church should be conceived and developed in an atmosphere of prayer. This is no less true of the bus program than of other spiritual endeavors.

Starting a New Bus Route

A growing program needs new routes from time to time. Some routes will grow large enough to be made into two routes, giving each of the two new routes a better chance to grow. Sometimes new routes ought to be started merely because it's good to grow. Workers may be found and routes may need to be created to give them an opportunity to serve. The creation of new routes tends to keep higher the spirit of excitement and achievement without which the bus ministry finds it hard to keep going.

1. *Enlist a team.* You need bus workers. Buses are no good without workers. Each bus should be manned by a team and this team should be composed of: bus pastor, bus captain (sometimes), co-captain, driver, and teen-age helpers. These teen-age helpers may be called stewards and stewardesses, helpers, ministers, or assistants. Thus, a bus team should have a minimum of five workers. It may have up to seven or eight. These people may be drawn together by the bus captain with the assistance and guidance of the bus director and pastor.

2. *Select an area for the bus to serve.* A more exact expression would be, "an area whose people the bus team will serve." The bus pastor, or captain, may first select the type area in which he wants to work with his team. This may be a low-income area, a middle-income area, or a high-income area. The bus director or the church's pastor and the bus captain may drive around through the area, study the environs to be reached by

the bus, and pray for the work. Then the final selection of an area will be made.

3. *Begin enlistment of riders.* On the Saturday the new bus route is initiated, all the bus team should be present at the church for the Saturday morning meeting of bus workers. Special helpers may be enlisted for this one day. The bus director, the pastor, and other members of the church staff may want to work with the new area for this day. The new route should be introduced to the group, the new bus team members identified by name, and a special season of prayer should be observed for the new team and the new area entered.

Graceland uses the door-to-door invitation to secure riders. Other churches use other methods, all of which are good. The basic approach at Graceland, used on the first day in opening a new route, and every Saturday for enlisting new riders, however, is *going from door to door.*

Teams of two are assigned to each side of the street to be canvassed. They are instructed to go to every door and to invite everyone to Bible study and to Graceland. The instructions include: smile, be very courteous, do not apply pressure, stand at the door to give the invitation. Visitors stand at the door of a home long enough to determine if those who live there are interested in attending at Graceland. Riders for Sunday morning are enlisted for the bus; these names are given to the bus captain so that he may stop at the home on the route. Before leaving, the visitor gives information concerning Graceland, the time the bus runs and returns from the church service, the name and phone number of the pastor, and other information the family may ask for.

4. *Keep the riders coming.* You may do several things to make sure your riders keep coming. (1) Keep them busy on the way to and from the church. Start singing soon after the first ones board the bus. Use Scripture verses and other means to make the time on the bus helpful and interesting. You may want to supply candy treats on the way home. Graceland provides money for this. (2) Upon arrival at the church, be sure each person

gets to the right Sunday School class or department. Special greeters may be used to take new riders to their places. (3) Every week visit each family that rides the bus. This is of utmost importance. Fail in this, and the bus route will begin to slip immediately. (4) Carry candies or little favors and give them when you greet the children on your Saturday visits. They will begin to expect this, but they will also respond to your invitation to ride the bus the following morning. (5) Leave a card, paper, or notice in the door if no one answers your knock. Your church may provide a door knob hanger or card for this purpose. Thus, your riders will know you have been there. (6) Keep high the enthusiasm of the riders. Prepare them several weeks in advance for the activities you will be doing on the bus and at the church. Show joy and enthusiasm as you visit them and as you greet them on Sunday morning. If you believe in yourself, they also will believe in you—and will enjoy associating with you. (7) Never disappoint the riders. If you make any promises to them, keep the promises.

5. *Work for new riders.* A part of every Saturday should be given to a search for new riders. The bus team should take a few minutes on Saturday morning to determine how many riders they want the next morning. Then visit all the regular riders. Then the team will know how many more new riders they should have to meet tomorrow's goal. Let them visit until they find that many—and more—new riders. New riders keep a bus route growing.

6
Bible Study Enlarges

While Graceland majors on multiple ministries, it also majors on Bible study. It touches the lives of people with its multiple ministries, that it may in turn introduce them to Bible study. With no Bible study the ministries would be no more than social action, good within itself, but not enough. But with Bible study every ministry becomes a service rendered for Jesus' sake and becomes a means of witness to what Jesus can do. This is what Graceland attempts.

The story of Bible study—Sunday School—at Graceland is itself the story of a miracle. Growing from 87 average attendance in one of the early years of its life to an average of 267 in 1968, 409 in 1969, 503 in 1970. By the end of 1973 attendance climbed to an average of 900 and in 1974 and 1975 to about 1500. A church that can do this can expect further miracles to follow year by year.

How has this growth been achieved? By an imaginative use of Sunday School methods proven over long years by hundreds and thousands of other Southern Baptist churches. Buses have played a strategic role in the growth of the Sunday School as have other ministries, but these outreach efforts have been related to the growth and development of the Bible teaching program rather than apart from it.

Developing a Staff for a
Great Sunday School

For every star in the sky there is an idea of what to expect in the Sunday School leadership. All of these are valid and have a place where they can be used. It seems, though, that there are a few of these that should be found in all leadership.

1. Positive Attitude. In the negative world we live in, it is difficult for a Christian to divorce himself from this outside influence and become aware of his privileges in Christ. Paul in 1 Cor. 2:16 (T.L.B.) says, "We Christians actually do have within us a portion of the very thoughts and mind of Christ." Nowhere can I find where Jesus was not able to meet the needs of the hour, whether to heal a man born blind or feed 5,000. Your leadership must be led to believe that in Christ nothing is impossible. To "doubt their doubts and believe their beliefs."

When "Miracle Week," 1975, and a goal of 10,000 in Sunday School was first shared with our people there was *not* an attitude of "*if* we can do it . . ." but "*how* can we do it . . ."

2. Enthusiasm and Expectancy. It seems to me that the same feeling of enthusiasm and expectancy should be felt in the Sunday School staff as is felt in a coach, his team, and his fans in the championship game. I believe if every teacher would come before his class with his sins confessed, and "prayed up" that he would not be able to contain his enthusiasm.

As we "wade" through the people on Sunday morning there's a feeling of expectancy that fills the air. Cheerful greetings. Teachers meeting their classes as they come in and involving them immediately in the activities of the day. Not dead, dull, dry, but caring, sharing, ALIVE!

3. Creative Minds. Out of the enthusiasm comes hundreds of ideas that captivate the minds of people. The person who confesses he isn't creative may be confessing that God isn't in him. Jesus was always creative, using that which was at hand: the twelve pots at the changing of the water into wine, five loaves and two fishes to feed 5,000, walking to the disciples on the water, the dirt on the ground to heal the blinded eyes.

In the same way his mind in us can take even the simplest thing and make it a "wonderment" for those who are participating. As leaders we need to ask God to give us creative minds to use for his glory.

This past year we saw our people respond by the hundreds to such simple ideas as:

a. Old Fashion Day—coming to services that day dressed in everything from bib overalls to the old-fashion long dresses. The day was concluded with an outdoor meeting in the country and home made ice cream.

b. Baby Day—all the babies in the nursery that day received a special gift and moms joined them at 11 and brought them to the auditorium for a special dedication service.

c. 100% Sunday—a month of visitation and signing up our classes preceded this special 100% enrollment day.

d. "Hobo Festival"—would you believe bean soup, corn bread, and onions? Everyone came dressed in their "best hobo fashions." There was a hobo band (combs, wash tubs, wash boards, saws, etc.)—and many other special skits put together by our people.

e. Pig roast—two large pigs roasted and all the trimmings drew hundreds of people out to the back side of our property for a special Wednesday evening open-air meal and service.

f. Staff Banquet—the staff (pastor and all his associates and their wives) planned, cooked, set up all the tables and chairs, served the tables, put on the program, and cleaned up the mess. A night of appreciation in December.

4. Evangelistic Spirit. Matthew 28:19-20 could probably be broken down into four points that are probably familiar to all of us:

1. Reach them
2. Teach them
3. Win them
4. Make disciples

It seems that the most important of these four is "reach them." We must reach them before we can teach them, win them, or make disciples. Reaching people captivates the minds of our people. In our prayer service on Wednesday evening, the majority of the hour is given to the people sharing what God is doing.

5. Goals that Challenge the Best. Goals! Challenging goals! Goals that are obtainable through a miracle. There is enough competitive spirit in all of us that when challenged we do our utmost to succeed.

From the total Sunday School to the little class in the corner room, there should be challenging goals. If I have fifteen on my roll, and am given a goal of ten, even though I have an average attendance of six, that still is *no* challenge.

We need goals that cause us to put total dependence on God to perform a miracle. Goals that bring out the best in us. Goals that cause us to stand on tiptoes of faith, too.

Such a challenge for us is 10,000 in Sunday School. Your challenge may be 50, 500, or 5,000. Yet each section has accepted that goal and is praying, planning and asking God to show them how they can reach that goal.

One of our members was in the hospital the other day and had on his "Miracle Day" button. Another person on the elevator asked him what it was and what it meant. Our member explained we were expecting 10,000 in Sunday School May 18. As this member stepped off the elevator the other person said, "You'll never do it." The member replied, "You're right. But God will!"

A goal that will challenge the best. A goal that will be a witness to the whole community as God works a miracle.

6. Plan of Advancement. "Plan your work and work your plans." So many times I have heard that. A plan of advancement for the Sunday School is equally important as a plan of action for a person. Our advancement plans this past year have included a week-long Director-Led Enlargement Campaign. Our leader was Leon Kilbreth who challenged us, motivated us, and led many to a deeper commitment.

Each quarter we have a high attendance Sunday with some

special day like "Baby Day," "100% Sunday," "Miracle Day," "Bring a Friend Day," and many more. Sunday afternoon picnics on the grounds have proved successful in reaching large numbers of people. Out of all these activities people are reached who for the first time find an answer to the needs of their lives.

"Reach Out," a plan of enlargement from the Baptist Sunday School Board, was one of the plans used last year. This is not only a plan of advancement but is a plan of spiritual growth for those involved and an opportunity for the teachers to use their creative ability.

"Hobo Festival" was a part of last year's "Reach Out." One section had a Spanish fiesta for the festival day. They decorated the room in Spanish style. One of the teachers is from Mexico and she supplied the food and taught the children John 3:16 and "Jesus Loves Me" in Spanish.

Plan, pray, ask God for creative minds and enthusiastic spirits with a willingness to go.

7
School Bells Ring

At Graceland school bells ring every week day. Our school and day care programs have opened new vistas of ministry to us. We reach many homes through the services offered by the Kindergarten, Nursery School, and Day Care Service. I believe these are programs that would add a new dimension of service to any church. These open up the possibility of using the facilities through the week instead of on Sundays only. These provide hours of Christian teaching and training for the children. These render a service to working parents by providing competent care for their small children. Many could not work were it not for this Day Care Service.

Mrs. Kay Barbour is the director of the programs and delights to testify what they mean to her and to the church.

Mrs. Kay Barbour: "To share about the school, I would need to share my own testimony first. When Jess (Jess Barbour is Graceland's minister of education.) and I moved here from Missouri I thought we were coming to the seminary. However, as it turned out God was leading us here to Graceland.

"Right away I began to look for a job. I had an elementary education major, but I had art as a minor. I could teach art up to the seventh grade, so I came to New Albany, because I heard about the school system here. We were in Louisville at the time. I was given a position; there was a place the school system had been unable to fill. I was an art consultant, what they called a 'floating art consultant.' I worked in several schools and as it worked out I had a seventh grade art class in the junior high school.

"We had been here only a short time when Jess was offered a place on the staff at Graceland. He was to be a missionary out in a mission project and also to continue his work at the seminary. At the end of the first year of teaching I signed a contract for the following year.

"In the meantime Brother Marcum had begun to talk about the possibility of initiating a school here at the church. I had no problem with it; I wanted to work in the school. My problem was that I had already signed a contract with the public school system and did not feel it was right to break the contract. I wanted to teach the kindergarten class real bad and when they placed me on the committee that made me want to do it all the more.

"I began to pray about it and soon knew it was what God wanted me to do. It was not just something I wanted to do myself. I called the school superintendent—my boss—and I told him about what we were doing in our church, but I told him I would not break my contract. If he couldn't find anyone to replace me, I would carry through. I asked him to look and to let me know. He called me the very next morning and told me he had found someone to take my place. I knew this was an answer to prayer and that God had worked a miracle to place me where he wanted me to serve.

"When I started the kindergarten I had eleven children, eleven boxes of crayons, a few supplies, and a place to meet. The first morning was really exciting with those eleven children, but what has happened since then is even more exciting. I have watched it grow into kindergarten, nursery school, and day care. The school has developed to meet all the regulations set up by the state of Indiana. Now we have about 280 children.

"From the very beginning our goals have been very specific. We have had written on all our literature a statement of our goal: 'We make no apologies that we are a Christian school.' More than one mother has expressed to me that that is the very reason the child is sent to our school. I'm pleased to say that because we've honored God, I know of no time we've ever been critized."

Some might question whether such a school can be a positive tool of outreach for a church. Must not the school concern itself only with the intellectual development of the child? Can it go beyond this to be concerned for the spiritual? The answer is that it can be an outreach ministry of the church. At Graceland this has been true. Mrs. Barbour tells of her personal experience in witnessing.

"You can't really care about a child unless you care about his home and about his environment, and unless you are willing to share Jesus Christ because he is the one who makes life worth living. Our goal as a school is to share Jesus.

"That first year I made home visits to every home and talked to the parents about their spiritual condition as well as the specific needs that their children had. Now we have after-school care, we have day care, we have kindergarten. Every home of the 280 children we have is visited at some time during the year and a visitation report is turned in. We can then make follow-up visits as they may be needed.

"Just this past Sunday a family attended my Sunday School class, a family in whose home I have visited twice already this year. I feel definitely that God is going to use them here; I feel they will be making a decision soon. I think of another home I visited. Doris Keller visited with me in that home that night. We talked about Jesus and both the mother and father accepted Christ as Savior and Lord. This family came from another background and did not come into our church, but the privilege of seeing them come to Christ was just as great."

Just as it is important to "hammer out" your philosophy as a leader in organizing a church, it is important to decide your purpose or philosophy in organizing a school. Without a doubt, it is of no value to have a church kindergarten, nursery school, or day care unless the following are your objectives:

1. to help children on an individual basis,
2. to help meet the social, mental, physical, emotional, and spiritual needs in the home; and

3. to minister to the home through the church.

With this in mind you have an exciting "adventure" ahead of you. Organize a committee of interested individuals in your church. Possible people to serve on the committee might include pre-school workers, a representative deacon, a trustee, co-ordinator of the pre-school department and two (2) interested members at large. Begin your planning with the idea of making no apologies that your school will be Christian. Teach the children to know Jesus and how to talk to Jesus in prayer.

Among the exciting things that will happen to you is the realization of the appreciation felt by families served through the ministry. This is expressed quite well by Mrs. Gerri Livingston, a mother whose child is enrolled in the day care program. *Mrs. Gerri Livingston:* "Graceland Day School has meant much to me and made quite a change both in my own life and the life of my small son. For the first time, when I go to work I do not worry about his being sad, lonely, and uncared for. Before coming to Graceland I used baby sitters—they were excellent but they could not give the love we have experienced at Graceland. Religion was a small part of his life before; now it is an important part of both our lives. I had never seen such warmth in a large body of people as I found at Graceland. Now we are a part of Bible study as well as the day school. We are growing spiritually as my son grows physically and mentally."

Working in the school program also causes Christian growth and development of those who are involved. Day by day the church leaders can see these people growing in grace and strength. Their lives mean more to themselves and their families and also to the Kingdom of God. Sandra Anderson, teacher and day care worker, relates what it means to her to be a part of the school.

Sandra Anderson: "In the late months of 1969 I became aware of a great need in my life—the need to find a new field of service. My children had grown beyond the place that they needed all my time and I had time to do something different. I began to pray that God would help me find the right place of employment, a place that would be more than 'just a job.' I had taught in the public schools some years earlier, but did not want to return to that.

"In January of 1970, I was offered the opportunity to begin the first nursery school class at Graceland Day School. In the years since that time it has become very clear to me that this was indeed an answer to my prayers. In teaching in this Christian atmosphere I have found a freedom to share my faith with the children and their families. I feel I have grown to become a better teacher, and I know I have acquired a new sense of urgency about the need of imparting God's love to little children. The satisfaction and personal reward I have found are immeasurable. It has been a tremendous thrill to see children and families changed as we have worked with them and prayed for them."

Organizing a Day Care, Kindergarten Program

If you have prayed about the matter and are convinced the Lord would have you operate a day care and kindergarten program, it will be necessary for you to do the following.

1. Analyze the needs of your community. Do you have a public kindergarten? Would a one-half day nursery school program for four-year-olds be of any value? Is there a need for full day care for working parents?

2. Present your findings and opportunities to the church business meeting and get approval to make plans to begin meeting the needs of your community. Assuming that you have a need for one-half day kindergarten or nursery school, it will be necessary to:

a. Begin taking applications of anyone interested in teaching.

You may, in the beginning, need to hire a Teacher-Director. Be sure to hire someone whom you have prayerfully considered and think will agree with your philosophy. Don't be afraid to hire a committed Christian within your church! It will be helpful if this person could be in on your initial planning and have a clear understanding of his or her responsibilities from the beginning.

b. Gather materials from other schools for reference and draw up a statement of policies. You will need to include such things as: your philosophy, the amount of fee and schedule of payment, calendar for the year (usually it will be best to operate on the public school schedule), the time of beginning and ending each session, your plans and fees if you provide transportation, and your statement of the quality of your staff (include information on degree and/or experience).

c. Using your reference materials draw up a registration form.

d. Study your facilities and decide what must be done or purchased in the way of equipment and materials.

e. Decide on an effective bookkeeping system and open a checking account. The treasurer should be a member of the school committee and should submit monthly financial statements to the church.

f. ADVERTISE!!! Use all available means—radio, newspaper, church paper, bulletin, etc. Inform businesses or groups where there are a large number of working mothers.

g. Enroll students.

h. Begin.

Assuming that you have a need for full day care, it will be necessary to:

1. Decide on your philosophy.
2. Contact the proper state agencies.
3. Make a survey of the requirements for licensing.
4. Obtain material from other schools which would be helpful in drawing up policies and registration papers.
5. Meet all of the requirements for state licensing.
6. Hire the required number of committed teachers for the children you enroll.

7. Follow the guidelines for your individual state.

8. Include in your daily schedule—breakfast, hot lunch, morning and afternoon snack, morning teaching time for all including kindergarten, nursery school for 4's and 5's and individual cots or beds for rest time.

9. Advertise.

Using the above guidelines, we began a kindergarden with eleven (11) pupils. In January of that same year we began a Nursery school for four-year-olds. The following year we had two (2) five-day kindergartens, one (1) three-day kindergarten, one (1) nursery school, and we opened the day care ministry. At present our school has grown to include two (2) five-day kindergarten classes, two (2) three-day kindergarten classes, four (4) nursery school classes, and four (4) sections of day care. The present staff of 31 requires a budget of approximately $1,300 a week and cares for a total of 280 children. This year's estimated income is $99,000. The school is non-profit and accepts no money from federal sources.

God will honor any ministry where he is placed *first!*

8
Everyone Stays Young

If age is a state of mind, and if youth is an attitude of love and excitement, folks never grow old at Graceland. Oh, they may lose their mobility. Arthritis may limit the use of their bodies.

They may need to sit more and run less. They may ride buses downtown. They may even live in high-rise retirement. But grow old! Never!

At Graceland they become "Keen-agers" and are in the "thick of things." At the church they sort of slide into the "Keen-ager" category around 55. The church has a ministry "from 55 to 155." The oldest person in the "Keen-agers" is 107! And there are a number of people in their 80's and 90's.

These people have regained a sense of expectancy. They have committed their lives to ministering to people, old and young and in between. This group in the church goes to the nursing home and ministers to those who are bed-fast. They tour across the nation.

They have a slogan: "It's not your arteries, but your attitude that keeps you from living." Their meetings are motivational and inspirational. The "Keen-agers" have a vital role in our church because they probably have the best opportunity of anyone to publicize our ministry. They have contact with more people than any other group. They have their friends, their children, their grandchildren, their great-grandchildren. And they have the expertise to add a tremendous amount of under-standing and wisdom to living.

One 90-year-old man in our church bought a five-year bond

on our building program in 1970. What optimism he had. In 1973, when he was 93, he bought another bond for our next building program. One day he was talking about getting out his violin and tuning it up, because if he didn't use his talent, he would lose it.

Our Keen-agers go to all-night retreats. Some of those over 80 years old have gone from New Albany to Florida for an adult family retreat.

Our Keen-agers are a vital force in our community in changing things. They have a voice in the political and social environment. Many of them have money to invest—we found that out in our bond programs. The older people were more willing to invest.

If churches would involve their Keen-agers in meeting needs, they would have a vibrant task force for Christ. And yet many churches are overlooking this fact. There is nothing more encouraging than for older people not to feel left out or neglected. They can believe that, in the words of Robert Browning, "The best is yet to be."

A church can create an atmosphere that will keep Keen-agers from having that "on-the-shelf" feeling. Most of them want to have a sense of belonging, being included, and usefulness.

Many times senior citizens resign themselves to do nothing. They tend to feel slighted and think that the world has passed them by. The church has a redemptive ministry to perform in this area. Our church encourages senior citizens not to worry about themselves—they are in the providential care of the Lord. We urge them to minister to others in the name of Christ.

At our church we never major on the morbid. We like to have joy. We stress the happiness of our Lord, the joy of living to one's fullest potential.

We even encourage the Keen-agers—widows, widowers, and Keen-age singles—to marry. I give them a "wedding on the house." Won't accept an honorarium from them. Because we encourage our Keen-agers to enjoy themselves and love life. If that involves marrying at 70, 75, 80, or 100, more power to them!

To launch a senior citizens' program, first of all, make a survey to discover how many people are in this category. Then, start out with an informal meeting that will include fellowship, motivation, and inspiration. Plan a program that will be refreshing and full of fun. Elderly people need to laugh and enjoy a good time. And they ought to have a challenge that will keep them going for the Lord.

Make plans for community activities. Ask the senior citizen what he can do for the community and the Lord. Give senior citizens full vent to use their God-given gifts. By opening the door to Keen-agers you are ministering to some of the most important people in the community.

The key to reaching Keen-agers is not in just doing things *for* them. Involve them in doing *for others*, too. We have senior citizens who have joined the prayer ministry to pray for ministers of the city—to pray for our ministry. And of our senior citizens, Miss Meyers has bathed my ministry in prayer. And really she is the power behind the launching of our church's prayer ministry. It was a thrill to know that there was at least one lady lifting me up daily to the Lord.

Let's hear from a few people who are involved in the Keen-agers program at the church.

Carrie Balmer, Keen-ager: "I am 86-years-old. If it hadn't been for the buses that come out and pick me up, I could not go to church . . . I get out on Monday afternoons with the Keen-agers and I have a wonderful time out there. I want to try to get an old man—he's 93—to see if he'll go to church. He promised me he would, but he's sick in the meantime, but he'll come and go with me.

"I have gone on five trips with the Keen-agers to places like Middlesboro, Kentucky, another place in Kentucky, then up to Brown County, then up to Rev. Rawlings' church; then up to Cincinnati, Ohio. The Keen-agers go on a trip once a month."

Jeff Barbour, Associate Pastor: "The Keen-ager Convention is an annual event held each August at our church. Senior citizens from across the country are invited to attend and share together in the day's activities of joy. The Keen-ager Convention began in the summer of 1972. That year we had over 400 senior citizens come to the day's activities. We have had the Convention every year since.

"The Convention includes such events as political leaders who come and share how they plan to meet the needs of senior citizens, fiddlers playing old-time music, congregational singing with print outs of the old music, personalities such as Col. Harlan Sanders (Kentucky Fried Chicken), handicraft exhibits, demonstrations, antique displays, and recognitions for those traveling the farthest distances and the oldest Keen-agers present.

"People from Florida to Michigan, from Virginia to Missouri have attended the conventions. Some of the steps we went through in preparing for the convention were: (1) secured a park in which to conduct it, (2) contacted all the senior citizens' groups in our Metropolitan area, (3) printed letters that our senior citizens sent to friends they know in all of the states, (4) intensive prayer for the event, and (5) contacted many personalities to share with the seniors that day."

Lucy Hendershot, Keen-ager (84-years-old): "About five years ago Pastor Marcum and Ed McCrary came here to visit with me. At that time I had no way to go to church—all I could do was sit here.

"Graceland was trying to get permission to have services in our building, a high-rise apartment for the elderly. The mayor told them that unless they knew someone in the building that would invite them in, they would not be able to have these services. So, I invited them in—this was the purpose of their visit.

"I had opposition to inviting Graceland to have services in our building. I knew that there would be opposition but the Lord led me through it. The first services were held in a bus out in the yard, but when the weather became colder we moved inside the building.

"There have been so many things happen to me since that

first visit. I have found something that filled my longing. I found what I was searching for.

"My first lay witness trip came about with my remark that, 'I wish that I could be a mouse and hide in someone's pocket and make a trip with the lay witness group.' Jeff Barbour asked me why I couldn't go, and I said I was too old. He and Ed McCrary talked me into going, and I have been to every lay witness trip since then. I no longer think that I'm old. I'm not as old now as I was when I was 40. I don't even get tired on the trips.

"Now that I've tasted life and love again, I want to live. I have no fear of death and I tell everyone not to fear death—I want to do everything I can for God while I am living!"

Robert Moore, Layman: "I recall when my wife and I became members of Graceland. The people from Graceland had been out working and sharing with other people what Christ had done for them. This I could not understand but, as time passed, I began to be like them. I started to get *involved.*

"I opened up the Christian Bookstore in 1973. Today the store is doing well. It gives me the opportunity to witness to other people and share with them what the Lord has done for me.

"My wife and I are the host and hostess planning trips for the sweet folks known as Keen-agers, age 55 to 155. Well, one of the ladies is 107. There is no greater joy and happiness than taking these folks on a trip.

"Ministries like this are why the church is growing spiritually and in love, because the church *cares.*"

Ministries for youth are imperative. The youth are, as repeated constantly, the leaders of tomorrow. But what about those who led in the past, or perhaps are still leading—the senior citizens? No church following the New Testament will cast aside its Keen-agers.

What is your church doing to harness their experience, background, intelligence, and wisdom? Pray about it. Give your Keen-agers the opportunity to experience *eternal youth* through Christ and his church.

9
The Handicapped Are Touched

Today a person could not talk about the Graceland Church without referring to its ministry to exceptional persons. Not only are they seen in the meetings and services of the church—and they are—but their joy in being a part of all that happens permeates the very atmosphere of the church. To minister to a special person is a thought constantly in mind.

When I think of our ministry to exceptional persons, I think of how it began. I attended a conference in Indianapolis and heard of such a ministry, to the deaf person in this case. "Do you have a ministry to the deaf?" someone asked. "If you do not, start one. It will be a great blessing, both to those whom you reach and to your other church members as well."

The idea captured my imagination and I found someone to come and share with us what was involved in a ministry to the deaf. Soon, as recounted by Mrs. Barbour and Mrs. Marcum in Chapter 11, our dream became a reality; our deaf program was underway. I had the privilege to baptize the deaf and marry the deaf. I was blessed as I watched the deaf "hear" because someone cared for them.

"Why not a broader ministry to all exceptional persons?" The thought came to my mind—a gift to me from the Holy Spirit. This was the beginning of our ministry to the handicapped.

Now Graceland has ministries that cover the city of New Albany and the surrounding territory. These include not only the deaf, but the physically handicapped and the emotionally or mentally disturbed.

The ministry provides Sunday School classes for these people on Sunday morning, some at the church building, but some at Silver Crest, an institution for children with multiple handicaps. The church has a bus that carries all the handicapped in Floyd County, of those who go to the county schools, to the public schools. We also have a wheelchair bus that brings the handicapped to church, takes the handicapped to the hospitals, and even a bus that is used across the Ohio River in Louisville, Kentucky, for that city's handicapped program. One bus in this program goes to Indianapolis weekly, carrying handicapped children.

So, the handicapped are touched—they have become an integral part of our church's ministry. And because someone cared, today many lives are touched, and many lives that are touched, touch others.

No ministry of Graceland creates more response or elicits more expressions of appreciation than this one. Week after week mothers and fathers and those involved directly tell the pastor and church how much the church and its fellowship mean to their lives. Mrs. Charles Murray, a mother, says it beautifully.

"I am the mother of two sons—one ten years old who is severely handicapped physically with cerebral palsy, and one who is two-months-old. Graceland Baptist Church, where I am a member, has been a pioneer of sorts in the area of service to the handicapped and disabled. For the past two years, Graceland has been a source of transportation for the physically handicapped children attending public school in New Albany.

"Graceland was one of the first churches in this area to establish a Sunday School class for the handicapped and retarded. I believe that the religious education of these children and adults is vital and feel greatly indebted to the church for this.

"I feel that Graceland is truly interested in reaching out to help *all* segments of our community and make available to them a place of worship and religious education."

With equally deep appreciation, Mrs. Muriel LaDuke relates how she feels about the care and concern of the church for her and her son Timmy.

"My son, Timmy, has cerebral palsy, cannot walk, and is in a wheelchair. He is a student at S. Ellen Jones Elementary School, five days a week, from 8:30 A.M. to 3 P.M. Timmy's wheelchair is very large and heavy; it has been adjusted especially for him and cannot be folded up as most wheelchairs can. It is impossible for me to lift his chair into our station wagon and the only other time Timmy can go, other than school, is when his father is home from work to lift his chair. If it were not for your transportation to and from school Timmy would not be able to attend.

"The driver of the van, John Schutz, has been wonderful to him. He not only has attended to his physical needs, but is very concerned about him, and Timmy has found a special friend in John. John comes into our home, wheels Timmy out and into the van, carries his tray for his chair, and extras he needs at school—then brings him back home doing the same. This is very helpful for me as Timmy must be carried when home in and out of his chair, and this saves on my strength for his other needs.

"School is very important for Timmy, as he needs something to do all on his own and meet and make his own friends. Although Timmy cannot talk either, he understands, loves to learn, and is learning a great deal since attending school. He comes home every day after school trying to talk about his day and what happened with his class mates. Although Timmy does not talk verbally, we communicate with his head shaking yes and no. It is also important for me as well; I have time for daily needs in and out of our home and some free time for myself. I can attend meetings and work for badly-needed new programs in our community for the retarded and handicapped people, not only what they need, but what is needed for parents and the family. So, without your transportation, Timmy and I would be confined to our home every day."

The joy of service comes to the worker; it is as intense as the joy of being loved, which the child experiences. Mrs. Margie Newman is one of the workers in the ministry.

She observes: "My husband and I came to Graceland in 1959. In case you're thinking only a large church can do things for God, when we came here it was only a dwelling house with a sanctuary built on a side and was using rooms for Sunday School. Very few people were in attendance. Later we knew we needed a church building and we stepped out on faith and built the present building. We prayed for a leader and that prayer was answered when Brother Marcum and his wife and family came here.

"I have served in many positions. As I said, when I first came the church needed teachers in the adult department, so I began by teaching an adult class. Then I moved into the Young People's department for a few years, then I worked with the first and second grades as coordinator, and then I moved to my present position. I teach handicapped children.

"In our church we felt a need; we had handicapped children in our church and we had just been working them in with any of the other groups. We found a loving teacher who showed a willingness to work with a handicapped child and we just fit them in any place we could.

"We began a class, just one class. A wide span, from the adult age down to very young children, was in this class. We had eleven or twelve in the class and we knew this needed to be expanded into a complete department. The church asked me to become the coordinator of this work. We saw we needed three departments, which we organized, breaking the work into better grouping and grading.

"Shortly thereafter, we had an opportunity to go out from this building to Silver Crest, an institution that works with multiple-handicapped children—children with more than one handicap. This institution attempts to train these children so they can go out into other institutions or into society.

"Now we have two couples who go to Silver Crest to work with children who are unable to come here. We also bus to the church those children who are able to come here.

"When we began our ministry we reached eleven children.

Now week by week we reach more than fifty children, some with slight handicaps and others with more than one handicap, for Bible study. We're working to provide something for these children through the week, for they have needs through the week as well as on Sunday."

Beginning a Ministry to the Handicapped

How does a church begin a ministry like this? Several suggestions can be set down on paper; it does not convey all the picture, but it is part of what is needed.

1. Let the Spirit of God touch your life. The Spirit's touch is required in whatever we do through our lives and through our church for the glory of Christ. This touch is essential in order to launch this special ministry to special people.

The people who do this work must have a compelling desire to minister with loving care and kindness. They must be willing to give an unusual amount of time. They must be willing to rejoice at even slow progress. The handicapped do not respond as quickly as "normal" persons. The workers must have patience and kindness. So, let the Spirit touch your life; work with these exceptional people that love.

2. Train workers. The training sessions should be in the church building and should deal with such matters as how to communicate, how to minister, how to care, how to watch for growth, and how to recognize growth when it takes place. Workers should also avail themselves of study opportunities on county, state, and national levels.

3. Provide facilities. This need is the same as it is for any and all programs of the church. No Sunday School can grow unless facilities are provided for more and more classes and departments. This work is a new work and must have its place. As is true of other people, these special people need bright, cheerful rooms that are theirs—not rooms filled with cast-off or wrong-size furniture. The rooms should be clean and beautifully colored, pleasant places to be.

4. Minister to the whole family. Usually a family has only one handicapped member. The life of the family may revolve around caring for that one person, however. When you minister to that person, you do minister to *all* the family, and include *all* in your plans. All other members of the family have needs and problems, too.

10
Walls Tumble Down

Mother's Day, 1974. At Graceland, as at most Southern Baptist churches on this special day, the church auditorium or sanctuary was filled for worship. At the later worship service, Graceland recognized the mothers present. The oldest. The youngest. The mother with the most children present.

To each would be given a corsage, and the corsages would be symbols of the love members of the congregation gave to their mothers, as well as an expression of the church's appreciation for its "mothers in Israel." But with a difference. One mother was white and one mother was black; they stood side by side at the front of the church.

The oldest mother had been baptized into the fellowship of the church at the age of 87; since then she had become a faithful member. The mother with the most children present was a black woman attending the church worship services for the first time. The service was more than another Mother's Day service; it gave unmistakable testimony that at Graceland walls have come tumbling down.

To think that the walls which separate races are the only ones to fall at Graceland would be a mistake. Other walls have tumbled down. Each fallen wall has opened new visions of opportunity to God's people at Graceland.

The walls of Graceland have been battered by change. At first, perhaps, changes in things that seemed small, but yet were important. Changing the order of service. Moving a piano. Using a business meeting of the church to air complaints that someone had been "tampering with the faith."

The idea of change had been greeted with a warm welcome. The lay people of the church felt a freedom to act. They knew that critical eyes would not be upon them, and that critical voices would not challenge their every move. The breath of a new day seems to bring with it change. Perhaps it would be as true to say that change causes the breath of a new day to be felt in the church.

Among the larger walls I talk about are apathy, certainly most difficult for any church to overcome. Even more is—or was—the attitude of looking at the little group in the church fellowship, rather than upon the city to which the group might minister.

"The way it has always been" has always been a tremendous power over the minds of people. Even when we are creative in our businesses, schools, and homes the one place we are reluctant to see change is in our worship. We are creatures of habit and to change is a painful thing for most of us.

The willingness to change may be the greatest change an individual or a church ever makes. When this has been accomplished—this wall has come down—other barriers or walls fall much more easily. A second wall that fell at Graceland was the wall that separated the church from the community. Even when the buses had begun and the multiple ministries were underway, that wall had not come down completely. Walls of fear and frustration can be as real inside the church building between "our kind" and "their kind" as they are real to insulate a church from its surroundings.

Up to that time we had been ministering across the city and some had been brought to the church from these outreach areas. Others had stayed in the section where the work began. Now the work had reached such proportions that many were coming to the church.

Many of these children had never been in a church service. They did not understand the reverence that was expected. Slipping out of a pew and walking down the aisle during the singing, running down the aisle during the preaching, talking during the praying were disturbing during the worship! Dirty, little fingerprints on the clean white walls of the sanctuary were not easy to love, even when the little boy with dirty clothes and hands did not know any better.

Then appeared in our sanctuary little black faces that seemed a bit frightened because so many others were white. "Now wait a minute," was the attitude of a few, "this thing called ministry is getting out of hand. How far do you expect to go with this idea of caring for people?"

We had spent months of preparing the people to get ready for such an invasion of the world into the "sanctuary of the righteous." However, you never know if people are prepared until the "storm"—then you see the honesty or the dishonesty of the commitment of "words."

The highest wall to overcome, the most tedious one to scale, the last one to fall is the racial barrier. Graceland came to see that this wall could crumble as the people fastened their eyes and hearts upon the ministries they could render to people who need the redeeming grace of Jesus Christ.

I shall not forget one evening in prayer meeting. I asked the question how many would be willing to accept black people into the fellowship of our church. Only two people in the service indicated that they would have a very difficult time accepting them. Two claimed they were not ready for such a move.

As we prayed and studied together about what it meant to be the people of God, we found a startling truth about segregation and integration. The problem lies much deeper than the skin problem—it is the *self* problem.

Our basic nature is to be self-centered. I am afraid of anything that will challenge my own little world or cause me to lose some advantages in the place which I have already achieved. You see, we have just as much a problem integrating the poor white with the well-to-do white, as we do the black with the white. The dirty hands of the white child leaves its imprint on our immaculate church walls, just as the little black hand leaves its impression.

We are not segregated from the black; we are segregated from the needs of people who are different. The person who sings too loud, makes a little noise because he doesn't know better, or smiles when he should be "dignified" shakes us up, too.

During our time of study and preparation for integrating our church with all classes and races, one man who said he was not ready to accept black members began working in one of our low-income sections. In this particular section he had to minister to all races and classes of people. As he began to see the needs and he was touched by the needy, he discovered that he could let a little black boy sit on his knee during a mission worship service with as much concern as he had for the little white boy who was needy. His attitude changed and he became one of the outstanding advocates of opening the church to all people.

Therefore, we discovered that to integrate a church we need not deal with a person's race, but rather develop a philosophy of what it means to be the people of God! What it means is to love people because they all are God's handiwork, God's masterpiece—the color of the skin, the place one lives, or the clothes one wears do not reveal the potential one has as a child of God. God created all of us with an unlimited potential to do his will.

Too many of us think like the little boy in a Sunday School class. The teacher had prepared the pupils for the coming of the pastor to visit their class. She had briefed one little boy to respond to the pastor's question "Who made you?," with the answer, "Pastor, God made me." The pastor came to visit. He asked the class "Who made you?" No one responded. The same question was asked again, and finally one little boy reluctantly stood up and said, "Pastor, the little boy God made is home with the measles." Too often we forget that God made everyone.

Christ is leading our church through the struggle of becoming the people of God. We do not claim to have arrived but we have taken a giant step.

Yet, one of the dilemmas we had to face was our reluctance to accept people who are different. Yes, we made all kinds of excuses why we were having the problem. "This strange influx of unchurched people is not reverent. The services are noisy. People of the middle and upper class would not continue to visit and join the church, if this continued."

But the one great truth we overlooked was the fact that this was God's work, not ours. When we do the work God calls us to do there is no possibility of failure. Fear of failure is the only thing we must avoid. Fear is not of God. We faced the truth that we were the redemptive body of Christ and he died to redeem the whole order of creation.

The people have come to realize that an integrated church is not opening the doors of the church, but rather *opening the hearts* of the people. When one loves, he loves regardless of a person's race or position.

Today our church is integrated racially, socially, educationally, and economically. It is one of the most respected fellowships in the entire city. This was not accomplished by bombarding the fellowship with fear and guilt because they were not including other people who were different. But rather by leading the people to prayerfully consider, conscientiously think, and willingly search for the true meaning of becoming the people of God.

But you are a chosen race, the kings, priests, the holy matron, God's own people chosen to proclaim the wonderful acts of God, who called you from darkness into his marvelous light. At one time you were not God's people, but now you are his people, at one time you did not know God's mercy, but now you have received his mercy (1 Pet. 2:9-10).

> In Christ there is no East or West
> In him no South or North.
> But one great fellowship of love
> Throughout the whole wide earth.

11
The Deaf "Hear"

At Graceland the deaf hear. They hear in the only ways deaf people can hear. Through watching the swiftly moving fingers of someone signing to them what the Sunday School teacher or the preacher is saying. They hear through the feeling of love and concern conveyed from the heart and life of a person interested enough in them to learn sign language. Yes, the deaf hear at Graceland, for at Graceland there is love for them.

The deaf ministry is one many churches should be engaged in. It requires care, concern, and willingness.

Mrs. Virginia Marcum and Mrs. Kay Barbour were in the vanguard in the establishment of this ministry. Mrs. Barbour describes how it came to be.

"I remember when we started to talk about a deaf ministry in our church. Brother Marcum had been to a meeting where the possibilities of the work were discussed and came home excited. To have such a ministry became a dream of his—and when he dreams of something it usually becomes real.

"Brother Cooper, missionary to the deaf in Indiana and Ohio for the Home Mission Board, came to our church and talked to us. When he saw that our interest was real, he initiated a class in sign language. He came for eight lessons. Then he told us we were on our own and to go out into the deaf community and begin."

Mrs. Marcum testifies: "I remember that awesome feeling we had when Kay (Mrs. Barbour) and I first went out. Only eight lessons! We knew so little. Could we even talk to the first deaf person we met? We took paper and pencil along because we were sure we wouldn't be able to make ourselves understood."

Mrs. Barbour: "Mrs. Marcum and I went out on Saturday afternoon. We went to a home where a deaf person lived. We pressed the button that lights up a light in the house to let the deaf person know someone is at the door. Nothing happened. No sound of a bell inside and no sound of a deaf person coming to the door, either. I tried again and still no result. I guess I felt relieved that I wouldn't have to try to talk with my fingers."

Mrs. Marcum: "Someone was there, however. He opened the door. We smiled, keeping our hands near the pads and pencils, just in case, and tried to talk. It was a little slow, but he understood. The man told his name, and as he 'signed' he became excited, ran out of the house, and signed 'follow me.' That afternoon he took us to a whole group of people. That's how we began—with Mr. Corrielle."

Mrs. Barbour: "But the first place he took us was to the home of a deaf lady, on the way telling us how interested he was in getting her to come to church. We didn't know it then, but soon learned, he was dating her. That's the way we met Hazel Ray. The best way we could we told her who we were and where we were from. We invited her to church and then wrote on our pad, 'We need you.' The best thing to say to a deaf person—or anyone else for that matter. That was all she needed to be encouraged."

Mrs. Marcum: "Mr. Corrielle was a member of a church in Louisville, but found it difficult to get over there. He began coming with Hazel, and soon our deaf work began to grow. Mr. Corrielle and Hazel are married now. They were married in a deaf ceremony in our church."

Mrs. Barbour: "Since that time much has happened in our church. Mrs. Corrielle has given her testimony twice in our church services through an interpreter. She explained that she used to go to church with her father and sit and read the Bible. She prayed that God would send someone to help her understand what she read. What a blessing it has been to be a part of the answer to her prayer."

Starting a Ministry to the Deaf

1. Contact the area missionary. The place to start with a deaf ministry is to contact the area missionary. This missionary, a worker from the Home Mission Board, may be assigned to one state or may be assigned to as many as three states.

2. Organize a group to study sign language. This group may be taught by the area missionary. Soon some of the members of the group will have learned enough to communicate in simple language and thought.

3. Discover one or two deaf people. When the first few deaf people are discovered, they will lead to the others. Usually they desire the fellowship between themselves that a church contact provides and will welcome the visits of church leaders.

4. Provide an organization. The organization may be simple. A teacher is needed. This may be a person who does not know sign language, but who is a skilled Bible teacher. He will need to learn to teach Bible truths in simple language which lends itself to easy interpreting. If a non-signing teacher is used, an interpreter will be needed.

The teacher may be a person who signs. He need not be a deaf person, but must understand the deaf and their need for Bible study in simple, understandable language. In most instances the teacher will be a person in this category. The teacher may be a deaf person himself, one trained in Bible knowledge and skilled in teaching his own people. Other officers may be provided the deaf class as need arises.

5. Provide a meeting place. This place should be a room large enough to care for the group and to make a reasonable growth in numbers possible. A deaf group may grow as large as twenty people; the room should be about the size to care for this many. Provide the room and leave the deaf group there. They do not like to be changed; in fact, they will take a change from room to room as an indication that the church is not vitally interested in them and is willing to give them a room no other group wants. If the group is moved two or three times, it may disintegrate.

6. Provide for the deaf in the worship services. This is a relatively simple matter. A specific place in the auditorium may be designated and a regular interpreter provided. Let the deaf know someone will be there to interpret at every service.

7. Visit all deaf people possible. When contact has been made with the first deaf person and one or two are interested, finding others will be no severe problem. They will take you to the others. Soon you will know most of the deaf in a given community.

8. Offer ministries beyond Bible teaching. Deaf people have many needs the hearing do not know of—often they need an interpreter. A visit to a lawyer, a visit to a doctor, a misunderstanding with those to whom they owe money, and other communication problems may present heartbreaking difficulties to the deaf. The leaders who are willing to help in these areas will render valuable services to the deaf and will earn their sincere love and appreciation.

9. Provide for social needs of the deaf. They love to get together. A deaf party is one of the most interesting events to attend. There is almost complete silence—unless the children of the deaf attend. If the children attend, a bedlam of sound exists, of which the parents are totally unconscious.

10. Continue training in sign language. Some who become involved in the ministry will drop out. Some will move away. For these and other reasons new people must be enlisted all the time. To make certain these new leaders are ready when needed, a continuing class in "dactylology"—signing—is necessary.

11. Vary interpreters. The deaf will soon learn which of the interpreters they enjoy the most. This person likely will be used most of the time. However, another person may be used to make announcements in the Sunday School class. If the deaf class is part of a hearing adult department, a different person may be used as interpreter in the department meeting time. Another may be used to sign the music selections in the worship services.

12. Win the deaf to Christ. All the work is done to the end that the deaf person may come to know Christ as Savior and Lord.

12
Apartment Doors Open

George and Sandy Penick first came in contact with Graceland Baptist Church through the apartment ministry. Their five-year-old daughter, Linda, was one of the first members of the Hallmark Village Apartment Sunday School class. This new, exciting ministry was the means the Lord used to introduce the Penick family to Jesus Christ.

George Penick: "My family and I were led to God and God's house by the concerned efforts of several individuals involved in the apartment ministry at Graceland Southern Baptist Church. We had always believed in God but had failed to make a public declaration of our faith and love through baptism. It took several visits from those persons to convince us that making a total commitment to God was a blessing and not an obstacle to be overcome.

"In December, 1974, we were baptized at Graceland where we received Christ as our Lord and Savior. There have been many changes in our lives since our baptism and we thank God for them all. But our deepest expression of gratitude is for uniting us with Graceland Church and its many members."

Developing an Apartment Ministry

Graceland began the apartment ministry with the firm conviction—we are dependent upon the Holy Spirit's leadership and power.

Two goals in beginning the ministry were (1) to glorify God by leading people to Christ, and (2) to get people involved in the local church.

The foundation for the apartment ministry has been, and always should be, the local church. It is not our intention to start new churches in the apartment complexes, but rather to eventually bring families into the fellowship of the church. It is with this openness that we approach apartment complexes.

Our present form of ministry in the apartments is children's Sunday School classes. We make no apologies for the fact that we are a Baptist church sponsoring the class. However, we stress the fact that the apartment class is open to all denominations. The teachers prepare at home, and the textbook is the Bible. We use Bible story movies, filmstrips, and flannel board materials as teaching aids.

With this open approach and because our church is known for being interested in people, we have had a welcome from every apartment manager whom we have approached.

We have used the same method to begin apartment Sunday Schools as we have employed to begin new bus routes for our bus ministry. We begin by meeting the apartment manager; he is the key person in gaining entry into the complex. We explain that we would like to begin a Sunday School class for the children in his apartment complex. We ask for permission to use the apartment recreation room on Sunday mornings. Of our five apartment classes, two of the managers gave permission themselves; the other three asked the owners for their permission.

Now the ministry begins. The main task is to spread the word to every resident. With the permission of the manager, we post notices on all the bulletin boards, above all the mail boxes, and in all the laundry rooms.

We have a portable cotton candy machine which we set up in the middle of the complex. We give free cotton candy with a notice of the new class. We also sponsor a free party for all the children in the complex. We show movies (which we check out from the public library), play games, and have refreshments. We bathe each promotional activity in prayer and openly announce that we are doing it because we love Jesus, because we love the children, and because we want everyone to know about the new class.

There is no substitute for door to door visitation. After receiving permission from the manager to pass out notices "door to door," we knock on every door in the apartment complex. There is nothing better than looking a person in the face and saying, "I am from Graceland Baptist Church. We are beginning an apartment Sunday School class for all the children in the apartment complex. We would like to invite your children to come if you do not attend church anywhere."

By using this method, we obtain the status of every apartment resident. We record whether the person is (1) a church member, (2) not interested, (3) willing to send his children. Every Saturday the outreach teachers go to their respective apartment complex and visit.

Each month we have an activity for the apartment children. We usually have a party similar to the initial party with movies, games, and refreshments in the recreation room. We also take the children skating once a month at a special church rate. During the weekly visitation, the teachers watch for new families moving in. Under the leadership of the Holy Spirit, we have used these techniques to help our classes grow.

Many of the parents have asked that we begin a time of Bible study for them during the children's Sunday School class. Our future plans include an adult Bible study class in every apartment. Because we have shown an interest in the people, the apartment managers have begun to call the church for special needs. We have been able to give food to needy families, help others with furniture, and provide spiritual help to many broken families.

The apartment ministry has opened the doors of many families to hear the saving message of Jesus Christ. Several families have been saved and have joined the church because of the outreach in this innovative ministry.

13
Material Possessions Are Shared

In the Book of Acts, the early church was characterized by its *koinonia*—a spiritual fellowship, a life shared in Christ. But the sharing was more than emotional and spiritual. It involved caring spiritually *and* materially for those in need.

For a church to follow the New Testament pattern, it must exercise concern for those in need, regardless of what that need is.

When God has provided for us, why not share our material things to help others? At the same time share love and concern.

What does such a ministry involve? The same things many churches do as afterthought—except with greater imagination and zeal. A clothing closet. A food closet. But beyond that, a furniture shop.

We have the privilege to reach out into the community and provide clothing for many families throughout a year. And because we have been able to develop a food and clothing pantry we can utilize and not waste the clothing that hangs in the closet and we can make it available to those people who have a real need. It has been a tremendous door-opener, as people come to realize that we care about others.

There is something about God's blessings upon those who minister in meeting these needs. We have seen many people come and select clothing when they have been "burnt out," or in the middle of the winter when they lose a job. When their children would normally go without the proper clothing, it is a joy to help properly clothe them. Recently we had hundreds of pieces of clothing given away. We ran an ad in the paper which stated that at a certain time we would be available for anyone to come and select clothing—no cost—just a ministry. And as people came we were able to touch their lives.

Daily we have food available. When we discover a need, we go into the home, find out about the need, and then minister to the family. It is hard for a hungry person to talk about "The Bread of Life," until we have put bread in his stomach.

When you carry food and clothing to a needy family, the door is open for you to share the Word of God—because they see that you are not only talking—you're living.

There is an incident which recently touched my heart. One of our church men had been out of a job, and one of our other men, in a very silent way, gave him money and helped him get on his feet. Many months later the situation changed. The man who had helped his neighbor found himself out of work for two or three months. The man he had helped months before one day slipped an envelope into his hands—with these words, "I want to show how much I appreciate what you did for me. I want to show you that I love you."

Recently we have added another ministry—we call it "Operation Furniture." We take furniture and store it as people are willing to give what they are going to discard. As families have need for different types of furniture, we deliver it to them at no charge at all.

It takes men and women who are willing to work to keep these ministries going. But we have found that as we challenge people that they do not have a problem keeping the ministry going.

When God puts a man on his feet, that man's feet become instruments of God to communicate the gospel. "For how beautiful are the feet of those who carry the gospel to the needy."

Among those who have expressed a word of gratitude is Mrs. Louise Cole, whose home was destroyed by fire. "About a year ago, me and my three children were burned out completely. I was new in town and I didn't know too much about New Albany, but I did know about a church named Graceland Baptist

Church. I gave them a call and they were friendly and told me to come on out, and so I did. I didn't have anyone else to turn to. I don't know what I would have done without the help of the church and its ministry. They gave me food, clothing for me and my children, and some furniture to help me get back on my feet."

What does participation in this kind of ministry do for the individual Christian, the member of the church? Mrs. Betty Seese tells us out of her own experience.

"I'll never forget the first basket of food I delivered. It was to a young mother with six children ranging from six months to eight years old. There was no father in the family and as I handed the mother the food, tears were streaming down her cheeks as she thanked me.

"I had never before belonged to a church that really cared about the needs of the community, and here was a family that had never been in our church, and we were helping them.

"A few months later my husband and I started a bus route in the area where this family lived and theirs was one of the first doors we knocked on. The mother sent five of the kids, but the six-month-old boy was too young. This family lived in our area for a year and then moved, but each time they moved, they still rode a Graceland bus to church.

"One of our buses picked up a teenaged hitchhiker one Sunday morning and invited him to Graceland. The boy had no shirt on and one was given to him from our pantry. So he attended worship with us that morning. He came to Graceland on and off for a year and one Sunday morning he walked down the aisle and committed his life to Christ. Had we not been able to give this teenager a shirt that one Sunday morning, he may not have found Jesus Christ.

"We had a 'Clothing Giveaway' day in January in which we put all the clothes we had in one large room and invited the needy to come and pick out the clothes they needed. People came from 20 to 30 miles away to get free clothes. It was a very successful day. In two hours time, we gave away thousands of different articles of clothing. God really blesses when Christians are free-hearted."

Initiating a Food, Clothing, and Furniture Ministry

A church has in its fellowship all that is needed for such a ministry of love. Here are some steps to follow in organizing the ministry.

1. Find a person who has a willingness to spend several hours in this ministry. A person who has a compassionate heart for the needy. Develop a committee that is willing to share the word.
2. Publicize the ministry—ask people to bring to a designated room clothing and food for the pantry. (Periodically this will need to be done.)
3. Keep a record of contributions that are made.
4. Keep a record of families that are helped.
5. Develop a Benevolence Committee to check each request for food and clothing. This assures the church that the ministry is not being abused.
6. Share with the congregation the blessings received from the help given.

"Whoso stoppeth his ears at the cry of the poor, he also shall cry himself, but shall not be heard" (Proverbs 21:13).

14
Church Members Grow and Develop

Nothing can help church members to grow better than involving them in ministry to the community. No two churches are exactly alike in approaches to ministry, I am sure. Yet, there are certain principles that every involved church will incorporate into its work.

Mission Action Groups

Our church works through "mission action groups." A man and a woman serve as directors of these groups. Under each of these groups are committees based on the needs of the church, the community, and the area. Wherever a need is discovered, the church organizes to meet it.

Generally, each committee meets once a month on what we call "Family Night." However, they meet whenever it is necessary for the progress of our ministries. The monthly meeting consists of planning the next month's work. Much of the planning is built around the needs that already exist.

These groups share creative ideas on how to minister. After the planning session, all the different committees meet together and briefly discuss what has happened and what is planned for the coming month, or even months. This helps each group to learn what the other groups are doing, and it builds a closer bond of fellowship.

The organizational steps are simple and have proven effective for our congregation. We have seen a tremendous growth, both numerically and spiritually, in the men's and women's mission action groups.

The steps are as follows:

1. Survey the needs of the community through a group of committed people or ask the entire fellowship to list needs in the community.

2. Use the nominating committee to enlist chairmen for the needed committees.

3. Call an organizational night. Publicize the meeting through all of the avenues of communication. Make this meeting sound exciting, important, and challenging—add some type of fellowship meal. When the night arrives for the meeting, have all the chairmen present and have someone to give an inspirational introduction to the program. Then give each chairman about three minutes to describe what his committee will be doing. After each chairman has described the task of the committee, along with the privilege and opportunity to serve on the committees, have a time of commitment and ask every member to volunteer for the committee of his or her choice.

This type of organization serves two purposes: it organizes men and women into groups that will minister effectively and gives each person the opportunity to choose his place of ministry according to his own personal choice.

The following are some of the committees we have organized working effectively: prayer; bible study; hospital; food, clothing, and furniture; bus; mission; jail; convalescent; shut-in; servicemen; out-of-fellowship; new members; housing; personnel (locating jobs); and many others.

Of course, the lives that are touched by these ministries are blessed, but another benefit to the church is the growth and development of church members. Does this actually happen? Look at some testimonies from some of the Graceland people involved.

Don Hardin: "I have received a great blessing working with shut-ins. By going by and just showing them that I care—by having Bible studies with them, praying with them about their needs and their home life. Just being a friend—taking them to the store, taking one person to the hospital to see his spouse, taking them uptown to do their shopping, and doing things around their home like taking down Christmas tree ornaments, etc.

"It has really been a blessing to work with these people. I found out that many of these people had spent more time in prayer than the amount of time that I had been a Christian. It has been a growing experience for me. I know the Lord is real—but it is quite edifying to hear how he has worked in other people's lives and how their lives have been changed.

"Another great blessing has been my work in the jail ministry. Visiting with the men in their cells, praying with them, contacting their families, trying to meet their needs. If they are lost, and most of them are, we present the gospel message to them. I tell them how the Lord has worked in my life and show them how my life has changed. Quite a few of the men that I have talked with in jail know me from when I was an inmate there, too. There have been eighteen decisions for the Lord in the jail ministry—four in one night."

Youth Grow in Ministry

One of the big problems we face in our churches is the dropping out of the young people from the day they graduate from high school until they are married and have a family. We believe one of the reasons for this rejection of the church during these years is the fact that most young people feel they are not needed and/or wanted.

They have not been given any responsibility. The church has always been trying to "do something for" the young people, rather than let the young people do something worthwhile for Jesus Christ. Graceland has the following plan to involve young people in service.

1. *Seniors in Service.* These are seniors in high school who are willing to go through the mission training program. They

are given responsibilities in the teaching program. They have classes or help with classes in the missions of the church.

2. *Bus Ministry.* Service opportunities for those in the sophomore and junior years of high school are offered through the bus ministry. They can serve as stewards and stewardesses. They are excited to visit and to render valuable service to the bus ministry.

3. *Bus Drivers.* Young people may become bus drivers. One senior in high school is a regular bus driver. Other young people drive buses, too.

4. *Sunday Evening Opportunities.* Senior high and junior high departments serve Jesus Christ on Sunday evening. They go to the convalescent homes. They visit shut-ins and provide services for them.

5. *Visitation.* Young people are involved in the visitation program. They are taught to visit and to share their faith.

A typical Sunday morning many of our young people are out early in the morning, excited about the possibilities of serving. They are filled with a sense of expectancy. They have discovered that God wants to use them, and it makes life more than worthwhile.

Our youth director speaks: "My office door burst open, and Mary Ellen Ragains, the minister of music's wife, stuck her head inside my door. 'Rich, Steve Merritt is upstairs and he wants to talk to somebody.' I knew Steve, because Larry, teacher of senior high boys, had made a visit to Steve's home only a few weeks before and had invited Steve to come to Youth Church at Hazelwood Junior High School.

"We hold services there because the church is just too full to have everyone there. Steve, to the surprise of us all, came the next Sunday. I had noticed even while I preached that Steve was troubled, but week after week had slipped by and Steve would not respond to the invitation. I had supposed that Steve was just too proud.

"Steve was a superior athlete at New Albany High. He was on the football team and wrestling team. In fact, he always wore his letter jacket to church and I had supposed that it would be next to impossible for Steve to respond in front of his friends. However, that Sunday night, Steve was upstairs. His head was down and he was waiting for someone to help him.

"As I approached him, I saw Larry, his Sunday School teacher, around the corner, so I asked Larry if he would come with us. Just as I finished, Steve burst into tears and threw his arms around his teacher's shoulders and cried in a despairing voice, 'Help me, Larry, help me.' It was only a few moments before Steve accepted the Lord Jesus as his personal Savior in my office. Steve is now sharing his faith in Christ with his teammates.

"It was this same youthful cry of 'help me' that I heard only a few days later from Leah Carr. Leah had come to Graceland on the invitation of her girlfriend, Lisa. However, it wasn't at church that her cry was heard; rather it was on a bus trip where she attended the evangelism conference with our adult choir. After Richard Hogue had preached, Leah stepped forward and Lisa came to me and said, 'Leah needs help.'

"It was this same cry of help that was heard last Thursday night as Leah took her Sunday School teacher to the home of her two best girlfriends. After Leah had shared her experiences with the Lord Jesus, her two girlfriends knelt and accepted Christ.

"The youth of New Albany are crying *help* and the burden to meet this cry is shared by the 'Graceland Young World.'

"A Youth Staff composed of teenagers meets monthly in an overnight retreat called 'Power Charge,' in which they pray for the lost youth of the city. The Saturday following the retreat, they move out on the city sharing Christ. At the last Power Charge, seven kids were saved in a shopping mall in one afternoon.

"Every Thursday night is for youth soul-winning, as the teenage Youth Staff moves out on the city again sharing their faith. Two teenagers were won last Thursday night. The youth at Graceland are discovering the meaning of 1 Timothy 4:12: 'Don't let anyone think little of you because you are young. Be their ideal, let them follow the way you teach and live, be a pattern for them in your love, your faith, and your clean thoughts' (1 Tim. 4:12, TLB). Graceland has many youth programs, but the central program is youth soul-winning."

My son, Steve, came home from his first year in college with little enthusiasm to just sit in a Sunday School class on Sunday morning. He and one of the laymen drove around the city to see what needs could be found. They discovered a small park in an out-of-the-way section of the city. The next Sunday Steve and some others started a Sunday School class in the park. They soon had a Sunday School class blooming and it reached a high of 30 plus pupils.

Steve was exuberant about his class and would get up on Saturday morning and visit on behalf of his Sunday School class. Never before had he been so willing. He discovered the joy and excitement of meeting the needs of others through the giving of himself. Today other young people carry on this ministry.

Another young person began to drive a station wagon for the outreach program. After a few weeks he was picking up more people than the station wagon could haul. He was promoted to the "Paddy Wagon," an old police wagon from Nashville, Tennessee. By now he has recruited two other young people to work with him and one other young minister. They filled the Paddy Wagon to overflow. Then they were given a larger bus. They really fixed up the old bus. Chrome tail pipe and Cadillac styling. You guessed it—they filled the bus with people. The only opportunity (not problem) they have is it breaks down about one time a week, usually on Sunday!

There is no stopping young people who are thrilled with Christ and his church! And no stopping of us "old folks," either.

15
God's Gifts Are Accepted

Graceland, as with most churches, has been built from the sacrificial giving of its members. They give of their time, talent, and material possessions.

A quiet man named Paul Wycoff comes to mind. He is sort of a shy person. When he first came to Graceland, he was reserved, seldom spoke. But he was around. Then he became involved in the bus ministry.

Before long the church would pray for another bus and ask God to give it to us. Paul would be out front, pledging $100 or $500 or $1,000. You may think this was easy for him. But he had to "dig," although he has a good job at the telephone company.

Paul never asked for recompense, never made any great "to-do" about his gifts. He quietly placed his money where it could minister.

I think again of Ed McCrary who is in the business of rebuilding engines. Ed, as I mentioned in an earlier chapter, has been vitally concerned with the bus ministry. He has given thousands of dollars that the church might have a ministry of wheels. On another occasion, when we needed air conditioning in the building, Ed put together custom-made air conditioning equipment at low cost. It works beautifully, although one air conditioning man predicted the equipment would not function at all.

Then, I think about Mike Trinkle. One day Mike and his wife, Lil, visited our church. They were members somewhere else. They listened to our organ which was, at that time, a small electrical organ. After the service Mike came up to me and asked,

"Would you like to have a pipe organ?" The thought over-whelmed me. At the time a pipe organ seemed like a "pipe dream"—we needed so much else.

Well, before long Mike found an organ. He purchased it from another church. He and some other men removed that big organ from the other church and installed it in ours. Mike, and others like Larry Tapp, spent four months installing and reconditioning the organ. That organ is now valued at $30,000. Would you believe that Mike is looking for an even bigger organ to be played in the new church building at the "Abundant Life Community."

Really, I almost hesitate to call names. Maybe I ought to simply run down our complete membership roll. I think about people like Hank and Faye DeFreese who moved from South Carolina and the Barnes'. Brother Barnes, when he first came to our church, was willing to drive forty miles to be our minister of music. He stayed through Sunday and visited for the Lord in the afternoon. Back then Bill's tithe amounted to as much or more then we were paying him to serve as minister of music! God blessed Bill and his helpmeet, Margie. Bill is now one of the leading men in a large insurance company. I think of Bill Newman, who is a giver and a "liver." He lives out the abundant life. And I . . .

God's Gift of Creativity

We did not decide to become a creative church; we decided to meet the needs of a city and to remain open to the leading of the Holy Spirit in accomplishing this task.

However, we were soon to experience most unusual opportunities to minister. Whenever a church decides to begin with the *people*, rather than the *program*, a unique experience is in the making.

Programs that develop out of needs are always different because needs are different. When this approach is taken, the church comes alive with enthusiasm, is concerned about people, and is involved in finding solutions to problems. Its ministry is as refreshing as spring showers and as challenging as the dawn of a new day.

Several long-existent programs of the church were not meeting the needs of the congregation. The staff and I started analyzing these programs. Why weren't people attending church on Sunday evening? Why weren't people coming to Wednesday night prayer meeting? We asked all kinds of pungent questions.

One basic reason people were not coming—the programs were not pitched to their needs. It has been proven that people will drive cross-country if they can get what they desire. The idea that people are too busy to attend church is malarkey. If statistics are correct, we have more idle time than any generation in the history of the earth.

The truth of the matter is that we do what we enjoy doing. We seldom get too busy to do what we want to do. Anyone can stop anytime and tell how busy he is. We never realize how much time we take telling how busy we are!

The reason people were not attending church was very elementary—they did not want to. We began to work on a program of "want to." This consisted of finding programs that were refreshing, exciting, and geared to the needs of individuals.

During Church Training each person was given the privilege of attending the union of his choice to train or seek new truth in an area of interest to him. I began an auditorium group called at first "The Worry Clinic." It was for the purpose of helping people deal constructively and victoriously with their problems. We later changed the name to "The Health Clinic." It was scheduled for only a few weeks, as all of the other groups were. Then we were going to change the programs. However, as we began these programs we saw a phenomenal increase in attendance.

"The Health Clinic," to my surprise, was destined to continue far beyond anyone's expectation. Scheduled to last for only a few weeks, it has gone into the third year.

"The Health Clinic" week after week deals with people's problems. You name 'em. We attempt to deal with 'em. We challenge the people to live victorious, overcoming lives through the power of the Holy Spirit. "The Health Clinic" has helped many to overcome wrong habits, has given new attitudes toward life, has made people aware that life can be beautiful.

One lady recently shared how her life had been changed completely. When she started attending the church, she was laden with problems that had defeated her. She had to wear a hearing aid in one ear. After attending the services, she exulted, "The power of the Holy Spirit has given me a positive attitude toward my problems." Today she is able to handle her problems, rather than let her problems handle her. And she no longer needs the hearing aid.

One man who spent many months attending "The Health Clinic" was able to overcome a problem that had marred his life. He had been in the mental hospital twice and he had to rely heavily on pills to carry him through the day.

He was helped to defeat the nerve problem, do away with the pills, quit smoking—which seemed impossible at first. Today he is an executive in a progressive company.

Another lady at the age of sixty-four was a nervous wreck. (Many people at twenty-four are in that condition!) She met Christ and was a regular attendant at "The Clinic." She was able to become a radiant "overcomer." Today she does not have to lean on the pills that cost her hundreds of dollars. And she has her "nerves" under control.

Another program begun to meet the needs of a special group has been a tremendous success. We decided to provide two classes to train interpreters for the deaf. Little did we realize that people would be driving many miles to attend these classes, so they could talk to members of their family or friends.

Today our young people have a project in progress to build a large teen activity building. They already have a sizeable bank account for the project. Young people drive from nearby cities to attend the church. Why? Because they feel a warm sense of being cared for and their needs are met. They want to come. When the "want to" is present, the program will have purpose.

What's wrong with young people? Nothing but a lack of challenge from older folks—a challenge for youth to give of their best to the Master.

The Sunday evening service has blossomed out with people attending because they desire to attend. The Sunday evening service is one of participation. The minister of music has the first part of the service for a time of singing together, as well as choir participation. All age groups from four-year-olds to "Keen Agers" have their times to sing. Laymen often share what has happened during the week in their places of service. Our services have become to a great extent lay services.

We are constantly challenging laymen to be ministers in the city. The laymen begin by meeting the needs of people. New ideas are always coming from them. They are constantly involved in creative approaches to outreach. They are not afraid to change. Or fail. When a program does not work, they change the program. They are not bound by tradition.

Our laymen have classes under trees, on doorsteps, in buses, in houses, recreational chapels, mobile chapels, high-rise buildings, service stations, restaurants, jails, convalescent homes, anywhere people are found who will respond to the good news of Jesus Christ.

One day a young man came by the office and asked if it would be OK to begin a class in his grandmother's home. We challenged him to start that week. Several boys were led to Christ in that home Sunday School class.

Our buses are used for the handicapped children, the underprivileged, organizations, clubs, and secular organizations. They are used by the Clark County schools in times of emergency, and by most of the non-profit organizations in the city. It is almost impossible to drive through the city without seeing at least one of the approximately fifty vehicles in our ministry.

One day I was at the ball park watching a game. One of our buses passed by the park. A little boy I had never met remarked. "Hey, there goes the 'rolling church.' " Yes, we have "rolling chapels" giving a vital message of Jesus' love.

A fabulous idea came from one of the laymen. He suggested we begin a Sunday School class in the area where his bus ran. This was to reach those who would not ride his bus. A teacher was needed to teach and stay on the bus, while others visited and invited people to this Sunday School class. Another layman who had never taught Sunday School before volunteered to help. God blessed the adventure of faith with tremendous results both for the teacher and the pupil.

Wherever the laymen find an opportunity to begin a work and provide a service, this is done immediately. No motion is needed; no second from the business meeting is required to start a new ministry. No "first," either! Our men just take hold and start the ministry.

One of our laymen is a living example of changing the locale of ministry to meet greater needs. He started teaching on a bus, moved to a house, and now is teaching in a city-provided recreational building. The building is air conditioned and a lovely place to carry on a ministry. This layman is noted for his enthusiastic approach to working for the Lord. He is a businessman, but more importantly he is a minister of Christ (not a "preacher").

A lady from our congregation started helping people who were in need of food and clothing. Out of this small beginning, with one lady gathering clothing and food, has come a dynamic ministry helping hundreds of people. One lady who felt the hurt and pain of others was responsible for this Christ-like development.

On a particular Sunday morning, one of the bus drivers rolled up to the church entrance. But before he unloaded, he sought a worker with our clothing ministry. This bus driver was carrying children from a needy family. They had worn-out shoes and ragged clothing. Even before Sunday School, those kids were outfitted from top to bottom.

One effective layman expresses his feelings, "I believe it would be awfully difficult to get me back into the traditional classroom." He said that with a smile and a radiance about him.

My definition of creativity is: taking that which is already there and remaking it into something which has the impression of your hands and has been brought into being through *the mind of Christ working in and through you.*

How to Develop a Creative Church

First, we must create an atmosphere where laymen are challenged to believe in themselves. Challenged to expect the realization of "impossible dreams." Most laymen have a reservoir of creative ideas, but many are afraid to share them lest those ideas seem ridiculous.

One night a middle-aged layman came by our house. He shared what the church had meant to him. He had attended another denomination all of his life, but he had never received the challenge to use his God-given abilities. As a young man he had aspired to become an artist, but was sidetracked by the Depression. At Graceland he was motivated to use his talent.

He began to do chalk talks for classes in the church. Soon his talent was so appreciated and developed that he began teaching a class to help others develop their artistic skills. People from another denomination attended his class. He did the story of the crucifixion and resurrection of Jesus in our evening worship service. He began teaching a class out in the city. Before his beginning at Graceland, he had used his chalk talk talent only one time! He exclaimed, "I always felt I had some talent God had given me but never used it."

Second, our preaching and services must lead laymen to believe that their talents are valuable in the kingdom of God. We must encourage them not to remain "spectators," but to become "participators" for Christ. Spectators never experience the joy of accomplishment that participators do.

An outstanding layman in our church had never even shared his testimony before a group of Christians before coming to our church. He now leads in public prayer, shares in the outreach ministry, and gives generously of himself. He recently commented, "This year I have made less money than last year, have given more to the work of the Lord, and have never been happier in my life." How did this transformation occur? The creative attitude of the church surrounded him with self-worth.

You've heard the old alibi, "When they were passing out talents I was behind the door." That simply is not true. It may be that you have put your talent behind the door after it has been given to you and not developed it.

Third, the church must broaden its ministry to involve the God-given talents of each and every member. Do not try to fit the person into the program. Rather, let his talents be used where they count. There's no use in making a cook out of a mechanic, unless he has the aptitude for both. The laymen and laywomen must feel needed and wanted.

The secret of developing creative laymen is to give them a chance to share—not only ideas, but also what God is doing in their everyday lives. Do not squelch their impulse to share with the church. Too long we have acted as if all the layman can do is lead in prayer or be recognized as deacon of the week.

Every Wednesday night we have "share time." Laymen are asked to share their experiences related to recent days. They are requested to be brief and to the point—but they are given a chance to share with others God's unusual blessings. Sunday evening is often a time of sharing in the service.

One layman explained what these times did for him and others. "It is just like the day of Peter, James, and John, and the other disciples. They must have come together daily to share what had happened. Maybe Peter had a bad day, and John was really on top of the situation. But when they shared their trials and tribulations, they all went out feeling more prepared for the task at hand." Now, a preacher didn't say that.

Finally, there must be a spirit of enthusiasm, an atmosphere of positive thinking, and the practice of positive believing—if you are to have a creative church. Negative mind-sets strangle creativity. They quench the Spirit. The question, "Can it be done?" should never be asked. Rather, it should be, "How can we do it?" It can be done if God wants it done. The word *can't* is not an acceptable word in a creative church. It *can* be done in the power of God's Spirit. God has given us unlimited potential and expects unlimited development.

Suppose the Apostle Peter had refused to launch out into the deep when Jesus commanded him to do so? We would not have enjoyed the tremendous catch of fish which was enough for all of the fishermen present (Luke 5). And we never would have read about the incident. Likewise, if we never attempt the "impossible," we will never have the marvelous sense of being part of God's miracle business.

Never forget that out of so-called "little" people and "little" places come amazing accomplishments. Remember Bethlehem and Nazareth. The Bible has immortalized the names of many "little" people, "little" people we would not know about were it not for the touch of Jesus. "Little" people who were made BIG because of Christ!

16
Dreams Become Realities

Dreams can become more than daydreams or idle dreams. Through the power of God we have seen fantastic dreams become realities.

We can recall the early days at Graceland when there was little ministry at all. I can remember when one of the men went out to start his bus, the battery exploded, and acid ruined his suit. A few days later one of our deacons was pushing *the bus* down the street and tore his suit. Yet, today we have over fifty buses, and the fleet continues to grow.

On my wall there is a motto, "A man is not poor who doesn't have a cent, a man is poor who doesn't have a dream."

How well I recall dreaming about a city-wide ministry. It was years ago on a Saturday evening. I was standing out on the church grounds taking a breather from mowing the grass. I was feeling sorry for myself and crying as I looked out across New Albany. There seemed to be no help.

But right then God began to inspire me—yes, the church is going to have a city-wide ministry. I began sharing God's impressions on my heart. Some people laughed. Some thought the dream would vanish. Some laid my dream to the misplaced zeal of a young preacher. But—thank God for that conjunction—others began to believe the dream. Laymen began to agree with the dream.

A spirit of enthusiasm and expectancy built up. With a handful of people we began to spread the word—and began to plan. In 1967, with the help of missionary Eldon Jones, we started house churches. We dreamed of having ten house churches.

Students from Southern Seminary would begin a ministry, and then move on to another house.

Out of the house ministries, we began moving toward multiple ministries. The people, through prayer and dependence on Christ, helped the ministries to multiply. God would lay a ministry on a man or woman's heart, they would recognize a need, and from the need would emerge a program. Need first, program after the need.

Today, we have a city-wide, area-wide ministry which reaches beyond New Albany to the "Falls Cities." A ministry that has captured the attention of the city and surrounding areas. It is not the name of the church that does it—it is the name of our Lord working through the church.

Another dream coming to fruition is the "Abundant Life Community." Perhaps this was rash of me. But one New Year's Eve at a "Watch Night Service," I drew some little circles and said, "We're going to find some land. We're going to build a nursing home, apartments, recreational buildings, a bus barn, a new church, facilities for the pastor, and homes for the staff." Just circles on the board—no money, no land, just a dream. Don't try that unless you have a compelling conviction from the Lord!

Our people began to look for property and to talk about the "Abundant Life Community." We found 36 acres of land which we were not even aware existed. Our people gave thousands of dollars on the land, and the purchase was made for $100,000. Today we have that gorgeous piece of land.

Only recently we have broken ground for a huge church with a 2,000-seat auditorium and educational space. Our "Abundant Life Memorial Garden" recently opened. We have two residences, one almost completed and another being developed. The camp development is underway and will open soon.

When God is behind the dream it can become a reality. All of his resources are at our disposal.

Finally, another dream. Meeting with Leon Kilbreth and our staff we began to dream about having a Nation-wide Church

Leadership Conference. It would invite people from across the nation for leadership training. In connection with this event, we would plan and pray for 10,000 in Sunday School on "Miracle Sunday." We would have the largest Sunday School attendance in New Albany or in the Metropolitan area, including Louisville, Kentucky.

We believe, and we have been taught, that God specializes in miracles. They are a matter of course to him. Dreams must originate with him. But God must have people who believe and then act on their faith.

Yes, dreams have become realities. We are looking forward to even bigger visions—to a nation-wide ministry. All glory, honor, and praise belong to Jesus Christ, the King of Kings and Lord of Lords!

We have written this book for one reason—to magnify Christ and to encourage other churches in their ministry for him. If this is considered only the story of Graceland Baptist Church, we have failed. The story is related in the hope of encouraging and motivating evangelical churches, regardless of denomination, to launch out on the promises of God.

ABOUT THE AUTHOR

Elvis L. Marcum has served as the pastor of the Graceland Baptist Church, New Albany, Indiana, for the past decade. Graceland is now one of the fastest-growing churches in the nation.

Rev. Marcum is a native of Jefferson County, Kentucky. He is married to the former Virginia Whitman. They have two sons, Steven and Alan Lee.

Marcum is a graduate of Radio Electronics School (Diploma), Campbellsville College (B. A.), and Southern Baptist Theological Seminary (B. D. and MDiv). He is a member of Phi Theta Kappa Fraternity. He was ordained by the Aetna Grove Baptist Church, Summersville, Kentucky. He pastored three churches in Kentucky before going to Graceland—Zion Baptist Church at Pleasant Valley, Macedonia (Ky.), and Greasy Creek (Ky.).

He has held numerous offices for his denomination, including moderator of two associations, Executive Board member of the Indiana Baptist Convention, Vice President of the Indiana Baptist Convention, member of the Stewardship Commission of the Southern Baptist Convention, and many others. He is listed in *Who's Who in Religion* (Marcus). He is used widely as a conference speaker, majoring on evangelism and multiple ministries, for Baptists and other denominations. He is a member of the New Albany Chamber of Commerce and is on the Board of Directors of the New Albany Drug Council.

SUGGESTED READING

BELEW, M. WENDELL. *Churches and How They Grow.* Nashville: Broadman Press, 1971.

BINGHAM, ROBERT E. *A Cup of Cold Water.* Nashville: Convention Press, 1971.

BISAGNO, JOHN R. *How to Build an Evangelistic Church.* Nashville: Broadman Press, 1971.

BISAGNO, JOHN R., and CHAFIN, KENNETH L., and others. *How to Win Them.* Nashville: Broadman Press, 1970.

CHAFIN, KENNETH L. *The Reluctant Witness.* Nashville: Broadman Press, 1974.

CHAFIN, KENNETH L. *Help! I'm a Layman.* Waco: Word Books, 1966.

CHATHAM, JAMES. *Preparing to Reach People.* Nashville: Convention Press, 1973.

COGGIN, JAMES E., and SPOONER, BERNARD M. *How to Build a Bus Ministry.* Nashville: Broadman Press, 1972.

COGGIN, JAMES E. *You Can Reach People Now.* Nashville: Broadman Press, 1971.

DEAN, KENNETH. *People Search Guide.* Nashville: Convention Press, 1973.

FOUTCH, FRANK, and SKELTON, EUGENE. *Involving People in Reaching People.* Nashville: Convention Press, 1974.

FEATHER, R. OTHAL. *Outreach Evangelism Through the Sunday School.* Nashville: Convention Press, 1970.

HAVLIK, JOHN F. *People-centered Evangelism.* Nashville: Broadman Press, 1971.

KELLEY, DEAN M. *Why Conservative Churches Are Growing.* New York: Harper and Row, 1972.

KENNEDY, JAMES. *Evangelism Explosion.* Wheaton, Illinois: Tyndale House, 1970.

LIVINGSTONE, CHARLES. *Using the Sunday School to Reach People.* Nashville: Convention Press, 1973.

MOORE, MARK. *Children's Worship Service Helps.* Nashville: Convention Press, 1972.

McDONOUGH, REGINALD. *Outreach with Church Buses.* Nashville: Convention Press, 1972.

NEIGHBOUR, RALPH W., JR. *The Touch of the Spirit.* Nashville: Broadman Press, 1972.

NEIGHBOUR, RALPH W., JR., and THOMAS, CAL. *Target-Group Evangelism.* Nashville: Broadman Press, 1975.

PINSON, WILLIAM M., JR. *The Local Church in Ministry.* Nashville: Broadman Press, 1973.

SHEDD, CHARLIE. *How to Develop a Praying Church.* Nashville: Abingdon Press,

SKELTON, EUGENE. *Committed to Reach People.* Nashville: Convention Press, 1973.

_____. *10 Fastest-growing Southern Baptist Sunday Schools.* Nashville: Broadman Press, 1974.

STUART, GEORGE. *A Guide to Sunday School Enlargement.* Nashville: Convention Press, 1970.

TREADWAY, CHARLES. *Sharing Christ Through Continuing Witness.* Nashville: Convention Press, 1973.

WASHBURN, A. V. *Reach Out to People.* Nashville: Convention Press, 1974.

WEBER, JAROY. *Winning America to Christ.* Nashville: Broadman Press, 1975.

Photographs

(Top) At Graceland, kindergarten and day care programs are maintained as ministries of the church. (Bottom) "Alpha and Omega" is one of many meeting places sponsored by the church.

(Top) Graceland is known for transporting those who have no way—not only to church but to other events as well. (Bottom) These mobile homes remain on standby for ministry if and when needed.

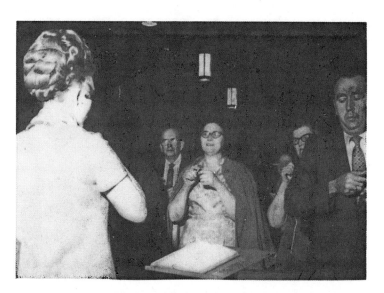

(Top) Sign language for the deaf is used at every service. Sign language classes are also taught to those who want to work with the deaf. (Bottom) One of many social occasions for the deaf.

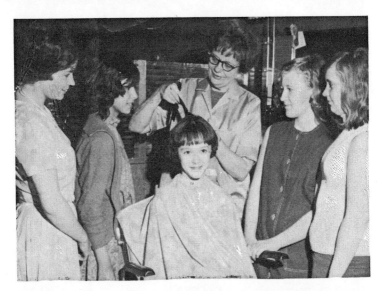

(Top) The church sponsors classes in grooming for young ladies. (Bottom) The church involves hundreds of senior citizens in Bible study, both at church and homes.

(Top) Smile for the birdie! You, too, grownups! (Bottom) The church has an ever-increasing fleet of vehicles. Here are part of them at the bus barn for servicing.

At Graceland every person is encouraged to remain youthful. Young and old are about to fill the air with balloons at the "Christian celebration in 1972."

(Top) You are liable to find Graceland's people having a service anywhere—even on a curb. Here they set up in a park. (Bottom) These senior citizens, and their young visitors, await the message from one of Graceland's laymen.

Pastor Elvis Marcum had a dream. And the people of Graceland dreamed with him. Most of the dreams are becoming realities. He encourages every church to have dreams and then to act upon them.

(Top) This one scene is typical of the joy that fills the atmosphere at Graceland. (Bottom) The director of Graceland's bus ministry shares his automotive knowledge with the church's youth.